Authentic Learning Experiences

A Real-World Approach to Project-Based Learning

Dayna Laur

First published 2013 by Eye On Education

Published 2013 by Routledge
711 Third Avenue, New York, NY 10017, USA
2 Park Square, Milton Park, Abingdon, Oxon OX14 4RN

Routledge is an imprint of the Taylor & Francis Group, an informa business

Cover Designer: Dave Strauss/3FoldDesign

Library of Congress Cataloging-in-Publication Data

Laur, Dayna.
Authentic learning experiences : a real-world approach to project-based learning / Dayna Laur.
 pages cm
 ISBN 978-1-59667-245-1
1. Project method in teaching. I. Title.
 LB1027.43.L38 2013
 371.3′6—dc23

                                        2013004309

ISBN: 978-1-596-67245-1 (pbk)

MEET THE AUTHOR

Dayna Laur is a veteran high school social studies teacher of fourteen years. During that time, she implemented numerous Authentic Learning Experiences in her co-taught special education classes, Advanced Placement courses, and mainstream social studies classes. She was featured in Edutopia's Schools That Work series and as a model teacher for Authentic Learning as produced by the National Institute for Professional Practice. She currently serves as a Senior National Faculty member for the Buck Institute for Education and travels nationally to train teachers on effective implementation of Project-Based Learning. She has a BA in History from VA Tech, a MEd. in Curriculum and Instruction from the University of Pittsburgh, and a MSEd. in 21st Century Teaching and Learning from Wilkes University. She is also a two-time National Board Certified teacher. She has written articles that have appeared in Tech-Edge and EARCOS Journal. In addition to Authentic Learning Experiences, Dayna's educational interests include the implementation of the Common Core State Standards and technology integration. You can follow her on Twitter @daylynn. This is her first book with Eye On Education.

ACKNOWLEDGMENTS

I would like to express my gratitude to the educators who allowed me to showcase their Authentic Learning Experiences. I am certain they will be as inspiring to my readers as they were to the students who were fortunate enough to take part in them.

I would also like to thank Jim Gates for starting me down this path all those years ago with his introduction on how to expand my virtual Personal Learning Network and make connections with educators from around the globe.

Many thanks go to Holly Jobe, my friend and mentor. With her support and guidance, through the Pennsylvania Classrooms for the Future Initiative, I discovered my passion for Authentic Learning Experiences and for training teachers.

Thank you to my close friends and colleagues Tim Kubik, Rody Boonchouy, Mitzi Neely, and Kristyn Kamps for your offered inspiration and words of advice. RB, I especially thank you for giving me the confidence to pursue this endeavor.

To Bob Sickles and Lauren Davis at Eye On Education, thank you for making this dream become a reality and for providing continual professional support throughout this process.

Finally, I am eternally grateful to my supportive husband, Eric Laur, who has put up with my late-night writing, been my at-home editor, and taken on the role of Mr. Mom when needed.

FOREWORD
by Holly Jobe

In an increasingly complex world where challenging, interdisciplinary problems face every sector of our society, it is critical for students to have the skills and habits of mind to be self-motivated problem solvers and critical thinkers. Rote learning and cramming for a test will not serve students to prepare them for their futures. Teachers are faced with the challenge of creating instructional environments that invite students to engage in open-ended, real-world investigations that promote critical thinking and academic rigor. Ultimately, the teacher's task is to be a guide to help students discover a passion for learning and to develop the drive to pursue challenging problems head-on.

The framework presented by Dayna Laur in this book, *Authentic Learning Experiences: A Real-World Approach to Project-Based Learning,* is a well thought-out instructional strategy for designing experiences to more fully engage students in their learning. With the focus firmly on student learning, rather than content delivery, this book presents specific steps with practical examples for authentic student engagement. The framework includes providing students with a challenging interdisciplinary investigation; linking it to authentic community or career interests; having students include rigorous research and academic justification of their work; showcasing their learning to external audiences and tying the whole process to academic standards and assessment. The Authentic Learning Experiences framework that you will learn about in this book can transform classrooms into dynamic learning opportunities for both teachers and students.

Dayna Laur is an experienced and accomplished teacher who, with ongoing reflection on her practice, has refined her teaching role to that of a guide helping students excel and accomplish more than they ever thought they could through the practice of creating Authentic Learning Experiences. I was privileged to work with Dayna as part of the Pennsylvania Department of Education Classrooms for the Future (CFF) program. She stood out as a teacher who used the technology (one laptop per student and ancillary equipment) provided by the program to transform her classroom. She added the technology component to a clear pedagogical process that she already practiced to allow her students to be fully engaged in Authentic Learning Experiences. Dayna was a model lessons teacher for the instructional coach professional development sessions and a keynote speaker introducing project-based learning. During the course of the project, she was noticed when she tweeted about her students' projects with a link to her wiki, and the result, after a circuitous journey, is this book.

This book is not technology-focused, and the author cautions that utilizing technology for the sake of using technology often complicates and obfuscates the real meaning of the work. However, she points out that using technology appropriately with Authentic Learning Experiences greatly enhances student independence and helps students develop technology fluency with tools they will encounter outside the school walls.

Many educators are overwhelmed by the demands to prepare students for standardized tests, or to meet what seems like a mountain of standards. Consequently, they are reluctant to stray from a set curriculum and provide open-ended, authentic, real-world learning experiences in their classrooms. Unlike other Project-Based Learning books, this one connects authentic learning and Project-Based Learning to standards (mostly the Common Core, but any standards can be used) and assessment. An analysis of a variety of sample questions from the PARCC and SBAC tests reveals a focus on critical thinking and higher-order thinking skills. With this shift in assessment, it is essential that students develop these skills, and using Authentic Learning Experiences is a good method for doing that. There are practical strategies in the book for using formative assessment to help not only students to be successful and actually perform well on summative assessments but also teachers to get to know the students and their individual needs better.

Educators know how important relationships are in learning. We need to know if a student is actually "getting it" or is sliding by. The strategies discussed rely on the teacher's need to understand the makeup of his or her students and their needs and interests. It is by knowing the students that teachers can guide them in their projects through scaffolding lessons and differentiating. Throughout the book, teachers are called upon to shift their practice and not do it alone. Teachers are encouraged to develop relationships with and reach out to colleagues and peers; to share lesson plans, assessment rubrics, and activities; and to get feedback as they transition their classrooms to vibrant learning environments. This is an essential aspect of continuous reflection and the building of a peer-supported learning community.

Using the Authentic Learning Experiences framework, you can transform your learning environments one step at a time. Start small as is recommended and you will be reenergized by the quality of student engagement and accomplishment that goes far beyond tests and will remain with students for their lifetime. I encourage you to examine the ideas of the framework and consider the many examples provided in each chapter. The project examples are from teachers working with different grade levels in schools throughout the country that can be modified to fit your and your students' needs.

By providing Authentic Learning Experiences in our classrooms around the country, I know we will be preparing our students for their future.

Holly Jobe is the President of the International Society for Technology in Education and served as Project Manager for the Pennsylvania Department of Education's Classrooms for the Future project from 2006–2011.

TABLE OF CONTENTS

CHAPTER 1
Authentic Learning Experiences:
An Introduction

1

CHAPTER 2
Creating a Challenging Investigation

13

Sample Authentic Learning Experiences

CHAPTER 3
Creating the Community/Career Connection

31

Career Connection Examples

CHAPTER 4
Justification of One's Work
57

Sample Authentic Learning Experiences

CHAPTER 5
Creating a Meaningful Outside Audience
79

Sample Authentic Learning Experiences

CHAPTER 6
The Common Core and Other State Standards
99

SUPPLEMENTAL DOWNLOADS

Many of the tools discussed and displayed in this book are also available on the Routledge website as Adobe Acrobat files. Permission has been granted to purchasers of this book to download these tools and print them.

You can access these downloads by visiting www.routledge.com/9781596672451 and click on the Free Downloads tab.

CHAPTER 1

— ■ —

Authentic Learning Experiences: An Introduction

Imagine a school where students sit in straight rows, facing the front, while diligently taking lecture notes. Day after day, the focus of learning is teacher centered. Test scores run the gamut. Many students receive As, but have they truly learned the material? Plenty of students fall within the traditional bell curve by attaining average grades. However, is mediocrity a display of true understanding? And what about those students who have failed? They certainly didn't learn the content or master any standards. How then do these students collectively perform on the state standardized tests? These questions have become more relevant as the Common Core State Standards movement has gotten under way. Finding answers to these questions should be the goal of all educators, veterans and novices alike.

I have always believed in active learning for my students. While there are times when I still need to use lecture in the classroom, being a stand-and-deliver-only teacher is something I decided to abandon early on in my teaching career. I simply wasn't meeting the needs of many of my students. In the early stages of my career, I found the only way to let go of lecturing was to create simulations for student participation. I tried to include a simulation with every unit I taught. Through the simulated experiences, I would have my students pretend to be members of an important committee convened in the classroom, or I would have them write letters to government officials that were never actually sent. These experiences, while valuable on some level, didn't create the spark of excitement I was seeking for many of my students. I needed something more. I also included elements of what could be defined as Project-Based Learning, with an open-ended question to be answered in an extended period of inquiry. In the end, however, much of it was still simulated, as Project-Based Learning encourages authentic-like opportunities but does not require full authenticity.

A few years ago, I decided that instead of simulating the real world, I wanted to bring the real world into my classroom. These real-world occurrences are what I call *Authentic Learning Experiences*. I'd like to take you on the journey of one of the Authentic Learning Experiences that proved to exceed my expectations.

My Story

While struggling with how to best provide my high school eleventh- and twelfth-grade law students with an understanding of the appellate court system, I stumbled upon information on the Cardozo School of Law's Innocence Project. I immediately contacted the Innocence Project to inquire whether my students could work with an active investigation. I couldn't think of a better way to get my students immersed in the learning process than to connect them to a current case! Unfortunately for my students, the folks at the Innocence Project weren't as excited.

I would not be deterred, however. I could do this one on my own. I picked six inmates from my home state of Pennsylvania for my students to investigate. All six individuals professed their innocence. However, I couldn't start with simply giving my students hundreds of pages of court documents to analyze. First, I needed to build up the anticipation leading to the investigation, and I needed my students to have the background knowledge to be able to complete the investigation.

I began with the PBS *Frontline* documentary on the plight of Roy Criner, a former Texas inmate who was convicted of the rape and murder of a sixteen-year-old. Criner maintained his innocence and was eventually pardoned after serving ten years of a 99-year sentence. The students watched in awe as the District Attorney, in reference to the DNA tests, stated, "I don't know that it's not his, just because they tell me it's not his." I had them hooked! And they were beginning to understand that "innocent until proven guilty" no longer applies once a jury has laid down a conviction. At that point, the inmate must prove his or her innocence, rather than the prosecution having to prove guilt "beyond a reasonable doubt." In the middle of the video, as all twenty-eight sets of eyes were fixed to the screen, I had a colleague slip into my classroom to steal my purse as it sat in the front of the room on a table. My colleague was dressed in a black hoodie and dark sunglasses. She did not cause a commotion but merely walked in, paused and looked at the class before she picked up my purse, and quietly left the room. Not one student reacted. However, a few minutes later, when I inquired where my purse was, only a handful of the students had even seen the purse snatch. At that point, I called in our school resource officer, a local uniformed policeman assigned to our high school building. He came to the classroom and took my students through an eyewitness investigation report. As you can imagine, the reports varied greatly. The height reports ranged from five foot six to six foot three, and the weight reports ranged from 125 pounds to 175 pounds. The clothes descriptions even included that she was wearing plaid! The point was made, and the students were enthusiastic. They were ready to investigate our Pennsylvania inmates.

Over the next several weeks, students researched the causes of wrongful convictions. They compiled their information on a wiki and completed case studies of people who had been released due to the efforts of the Innocence Project. At that point, they were ready to dive into their own investigations. The class was divided into groups, and each group was given an inmate to investigate. They read court documents and conducted phone interviews with people involved in the original investigation. In one case, a group of students was invited into the home of the parents of a slain child; the couple's older son had been convicted of the killing. I was amazed, and the students were truly involved in an Authentic Learning Experience!

As the investigations progressed, each group was able to choose the manner in which it could bring attention to the plight of its assigned inmate. In one case, the students decided the inmate was rightfully convicted. This group of students created a general action plan on behalf of all wrongfully convicted inmates and sent their ideas to our local state representative. In the other cases, the action plans ranged from writing a letter to the governor to creating a plan for a new TV show that they pitched to *Investigation Discovery*. Another group of students was disappointed that *Dateline NBC* didn't respond to their request to feature their inmate on a show. The governor did respond to a group. Much to the students' dismay, however, the response included the fact that, as governor, he was powerless to do anything about the case per the Pennsylvania Constitution. The Pennsylvania

Board of Pardons would have to be contacted and the appropriate forms completed. Thus, the very next semester, another group took up the plight of inmate Noel Montalvo and sent him a letter requesting that he complete the forms. While I was certain that his lawyer had probably taken this very same action at some point, I allowed the students to follow their own plan. Amazingly enough, three months later, I received a letter from Greene Correctional Institute, Death Row. It was addressed to "The Law Teacher at Central York High School." I tracked down the only group member who hadn't yet graduated, and she read the letter in awe and amazement. Montalvo had responded to them! The letter was typed and in broken English, but it included the latest forensic investigation on his case. It reported a possible mistake in the original investigation and named a local detective, who just happened to be a football coach in our district, as one of the main players in his conviction. The student was amazed! Montalvo also thanked the students for wanting to help: "I appreciate your interest in my particular case, and I need your help to exonerate me."

While my quest for an Authentic Learning Experience for my students initially reached a roadblock from the Innocence Project, I quickly found that I didn't need the organization's help. I created my own Innocence Authentic Learning Experience for my students. While my students were unable to actually see any of their efforts realized, the lessons learned from the experience won't soon be forgotten. My hope is that all students are given the opportunity to engage in these kinds of experiences and that the classroom meets the real world more often.

Unlike the scenario described in the opening paragraph of this chapter, my Innocence Authentic Learning Experience had me relinquish much of my control of the classroom, turning it over to the students. I became the facilitator of my students' learning, while my students became the directors of their own learning experience. Learning, in my classroom, is no longer categorized as a "one size fits all" model.

Figure 1.1 (page 5) summarizes the effective elements I've determined need to be part of Authentic Learning Experiences. We'll discuss each element in the next sections.

An Overview of Authentic Learning Experiences

Give a student an assignment that is too easy, and the student quickly becomes disengaged. Conversely, give a student an assignment that is too difficult, and frustration is quickly exhibited. Providing students with a *challenging investigation* in an Authentic Learning Experience is impera-

Figure 1.1   Elements of Authentic Learning Experiences

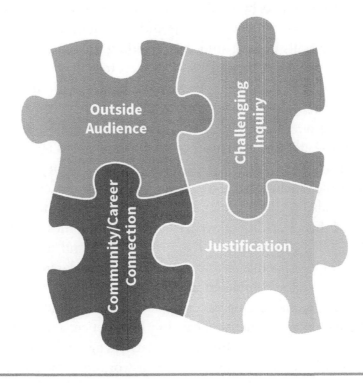

AUTHENTIC LEARNING EXPERIENCES

tive for student engagement. This process must be tailored to create a desire for students to dig deeply into the course content and standards of learning. Students in today's classroom must be presented with complex problems and challenges to solve. These challenges are action oriented in nature and leave the philosophical questions to be contextualized within the process of the challenging investigation. Additionally, these challenges are not designed to be simulated experiences in which students pretend to be experts in their field of study. These challenges revolve around open-ended, real-world questions that promote critical thinking. In fact, implementing a particular Authentic Learning Experience with one group of students might produce totally different results than with another group of students. Different students bring different learning styles and distinctive background experiences that may impact how they go about solving the challenging investigation. In any case, the application of critical-thinking skills to solve the challenging investigation creates a culture of engagement and promotes a deep understanding of the core content and standards for learning.

As we enter the age of the Common Core State Standards and assessments, we know critical thinking is a necessary 21st-century skill that must be honed and developed by students. To facilitate this, teachers can first model the process of critical thinking and then monitor and assess the critical-thinking skills of each student. Providing the opportunity to think critically about the course content and apply it to new situations prepares students to actively engage in the Authentic Learning Experience.

There has been much discussion of, and concern with, how to reach 21st-century learners and how to teach them 21st-century skills. Involving students in Authentic Learning Experiences engages students in their own learning and helps them develop essential 21st-century competencies. These skills, which include critical thinking, collaboration, communication, and creativity, also provide students with the framework to contextualize or understand their learning experiences. Developing these skills prepares students for college, career, and other parts of life, and for viewing their education in the perspective of the world outside the classroom, instead of just as an exercise to be completed in the classroom.

Formulating a challenging investigation is the first step in the design process of creating an Authentic Learning Experience, and Chapter 2 will explain this in more detail. While many teachers agree that students need to experience the real world, replicating real-world experiences within the classroom can be tricky. More often than not, an "authentic-like" project is created for students to complete. This is a simulated experience in the classroom that is graded by the teacher and simply returned to the student. These authentic-like projects or activities may require students to think critically. They may also challenge the students to go beyond the simple memorization of content. In some instances, the simulated experience may engage many of the students in their own learning. However, these simulated experiences fall short.

In a simulated classroom experience, the connection between the content in question and the student is easily lost. While the simulation may engage the students, in whole or in part, the relevance to the lives of the students is rarely apparent. In fact, the relevance to the lives of the students may not even be apparent to the teacher. The simulation is most frequently designed to require active learning by the student as opposed to the passive consumption of content. This does have a place in the classroom and can be used as an effective scaffolding strategy. However, to use a simulated extended activity in lieu of an Authentic Learning Experience often leaves behind the relevance and the meaning of the content to the student. Figure 1.2 (below) shows the differences between simulated projects and Authentic Learning Experiences.

Figure 1.2   Differences Between Simulations and Authentic Learning Experiences

SIMULATIONS	AUTHENTIC LEARNING EXPERIENCES
Let's pretend	Purpose driven
Activity based	Extended learning
Content knowledge application is limited	Promotes depth of knowledge throughout the process
Read about experts	Expert involvement
Replication	Innovation
Classroom production	Community or global audience
Focus on teacher assessment	Focus on audience assessment
Engagement often limited to grading outcome	Increased engagement due to purpose, need, and meaning

Designing a challenging investigation around a *community or career connection* creates a correlation between the course content and standards and the lives of the students. The challenging investigation could be linked directly to the school community or local community, could be designed around a debatable state problem, could focus on a pressing national or foreign issue, or could involve exploring a potential career. Whatever the focus, this element is directly tied to the challenging investigation, so it goes beyond the simple service-learning opportunities that are often provided as senior projects or as after-school activities. The community/career connection increases student motivation for learning, and Chapter 3 will explore this in more detail. No longer is the material simply something to be memorized from a textbook, but it is relevant and engaging for the students. This element takes away the "Why do I need to know this?" question. It is also strongly tied to the 21st-century skill of collaboration, as it is necessary for students to work collectively with one another and possibly with experts to explore the challenging investigation.

The community/career connection can be used in all content areas. While most teachers would readily agree that social studies content is easily tied to this element, teachers of other content areas may have to stretch to master making this connection. However, the connection is there for all content areas that incorporate both core and special subjects, including everything from health and physical education to art and foreign languages.

Example challenging investigations that include a focus on one or more content areas and could be adapted for multiple grade levels might ask students to investigate and propose answers for any of the questions shown in Figure 1.3 (below).

Figure 1.3 Creating a Community Connection at All Levels

CHALLENGING INVESTIGATION	COMMUNITY CONNECTION	POSSIBLE CONTENT AREAS	POSSIBLE GRADE LEVELS
How can we design a community park for a vacant lot that will attract investors?	Local	Math ELA Physical education Business	Elementary Middle High
How can we persuade state lawmakers to increase funding for the arts in public education?	State	Art Social studies ELA	Upper elementary Middle High
How can we create a plan to make domestic airline travel more efficient?	National	Math ELA Science	Middle High
How can we create a plan to completely withdraw U.S. troops from foreign occupation by the end of the fiscal year?	Global	Statistics ELA Social studies	Middle High
How can we design and run a successful preschool at our high school?	Career	Psychology Business ELA FCS (Family Consumer Science)	High

Frequently, students produce work in which they apply critical-thinking skills in order to solve a complex problem or challenge. However, rarely do students need to defend or justify their answers. In fact, often students are merely faced with answering a question or solving a problem that has only one right answer. Accordingly, the third element of the framework centers on a *justification* for the solutions and proposals created in response to the challenging investigation. Students again must use critical-thinking skills and focus on depth of content knowledge in order to defend any proposed solutions. This framework is grounded in content knowledge, an element that many educators fear is left out of any methodology that is student centered. In this justification phase, which is detailed in Chapter 4, students use research and interactions with professionals as they support their solutions. Students may use the results from polls they have administered or interviews with field professionals they have conducted as part of their justification for their solutions, designs, or proposals. Additionally, this phase requires students to go beyond merely writing a research paper to support a thesis statement. Students now not only consume the information but also produce new meaning from that information.

Traditionally, schoolwork is created for classroom use only. Rarely do student products reach beyond the eyes and ears of the classroom teacher and classmates. Occasionally, an end product is put on exhibit in the school display case or is produced for judging at the science fair. However, in most cases, there is little to no incentive for students to produce work that is done in a professional manner. Therefore, a critical fourth element to the Authentic Learning Experience framework is ensuring that the proposals, possible solutions, or end products are presented to an *outside audience*. This means going beyond the classroom walls, beyond just teachers and peers. This element promotes the 21st-century skill of communication.

The use of an outside audience, which is the focus of Chapter 5, can be mastered in a variety of contexts. Students can participate in a formal presentation to a panel of professionals or simply write a letter to a legislator or professional organization. Student work can be put on display at the local library or submitted to a journal publication. Perhaps the challenging investigation might lead students to initiate fund-raising efforts for a charitable organization. Additionally, with the endless possibilities presented via technology, students can submit their work online to a professional halfway across the world for review. Figure 1.4 (page 10) shows sample outside audiences for the challenging investigation questions listed in Figure 1.3.

Each of the Authentic Learning Experience elements connects back to the Common Core State Standards. At the heart of any good framework should be standards. The Common Core State Standards are intended as a guide to ensure all students across the country are prepared for both a collegiate and a career pathway. In both pathways, students will be presented

Figure 1.4   Sample Outside Audiences

- A panel of community leaders and business partners, such as the mayor and the head of the town's planning commission, listen to the formal presentation.
- Letters are written and sent to a variety of state lawmakers, including the local state representatives and senator for the school district.
- A presentation is made to airline executives or airport officials or, if these experts can't be secured for a formal presentation, Web 2.0 tools are utilized to create the plan and send it to the aforementioned experts.
- A U.S. solider who is currently deployed overseas, who has previously Skyped with the students, is now the reviewer of the proposals via any Web 2.0 tool, such as Prezi.
- A panel that consists of certified and licensed early childhood professionals reviews the design of the potential preschool.

with situations and demands that require a mastery of the inquiry process. Therefore, it is imperative that as educators, we prepare our students and allow them to hone their inquiry skills while they are still in our classrooms. It, too, should be noted that the few states such as Texas and Alaska that have not adopted the Common Core State Standards are not left out of this instructional model. Standards, no matter what standards, are imperative guides for designing curriculum and the lessons used to support them.

In Authentic Learning Experiences, standards, whether they are local, state, or national standards, should promote what students know and be able to do. As the Common Core State Standards were created with authenticity in mind, so must be the design of our curriculum and the implementation of that curriculum. Using these standards as a foundation for the conception of the learning in which students will engage in your classroom is necessary no matter what the chosen methodology of implementation. However, using Authentic Learning Experiences, which are rooted in the standards, will not only ensure students truly grasp the critical content but also that they are invested in their own mastery of learning and the exhibition of that learning. A more detailed exploration of the connection to the standards is provided in Chapter 6.

Keep in mind that technology is not a requirement for an Authentic Learning Experience. In fact, while technology certainly serves to enhance the global connections that may be made or create a link to an outside audience, the mere use of technology does not indicate a well-designed experience for students. Utilizing technology for the sake of technology does nothing more than complicate the educational process, as often the real meaning behind the standards and content is lost on our students. Teachers might focus an effort on building a website that is visually appealing or designing a wiki full of content, but that does not necessarily mean there has been a deliberate focus on the promotion of critical-thinking skills or on solving real-world problems. Thus, I have featured some examples of Authentic Learning Experiences in this book that include technology and others that completely rely on nontechnological means. I think, however, that as we increasingly have the technology capabilities at hand, we must determine ways in which we can appropriately incorporate technology in a seamless manner into the design of our Authentic Learning Experiences. While I could provide you with many reasons why I truly believe this is imperative, rather I will let you ponder the words of Ibrahim Kamara, a former child soldier and a strong supporter of the Empowering Children and Youth School that is discussed in Chapter 4.

> The classroom in Sierra Leone is different from the western classroom. We depend on textbooks, chalk and blackboards, which help make our children understand. This has stuck our children in a thinking of the old classroom system. The old classroom system is a disconnection when it comes to exploring global issues and solving real world problems. Technology is not present in the classroom in Sierra Leone. Only a few schools of the top schools in Freetown are trying to bring technology in their schools, where the students can access it once or twice per week, but yet the message is not clear. These schools [that] have the facilities are still struggling to use the tools to bring in better learning. Secondary students must have more chances to explore the technology age and must be able to use technology to solve class problems. All their answers are there. (Kamara, as written to his colleague Ben Stern)

Join me in this journey of learning how to design Authentic Learning Experiences. Each chapter includes example ideas for you to further refine and develop. Additionally, a more detailed elementary, middle, and high school example is provided in each of these design chapters. While each chapter focuses more specifically on one of the elements of Authentic Learning Experiences, I have provided an explanation of each element in these detailed examples in order to give you a better sense of the overall picture of each experience.

I encourage you to investigate the variety of grade levels and content areas and note the range of schools used based on regions, demographics, and type (for example, traditional public, charter, and private). Take the ideas that are provided and modify them to fit the needs of your students. Adapt the grade-level examples to be appropriate for your own. Discover how to take these experiences and effectively implement them in your own classes as you formatively assess your students to provide differentiation as needed. Transform your teaching and transform the lives of your students as your classroom gains meaning and your students bring about community change.

CHAPTER 2

— ■ —

Creating a Challenging Investigation

Students often find conducting research to be a laborious task. The dreaded research paper is not something a student looks forward to completing, nor is it something a teacher looks forward to grading! However, learning how to research is a needed skill for students. Teachers must determine the ways in which researching skills are mastered to help students move beyond the mere regurgitation of information. Therefore, students are not only able to be consumers of information but are also able to be producers of new information that has been analyzed, evaluated, and applied.

In today's world of Web 2.0, we need to ask ourselves, "Can my students Google the answer to this question?" If they can Google it, what's the point? Sure, we need to instruct our students on the proper techniques for conducting valid research, both online and in print. However, we must prompt our students to go beyond simple surface research. We need to create a challenging investigation for them to complete.

Complex Problems

The world around us presents many problems for which we have yet to determine viable solutions. Check out InnoCentive to note just a few of these gripping problems! (See Figure 2.1, page 14.) InnoCentive is a self-described "leader in crowdsourcing [outsourcing of a task/problem to an undefined group of people] innovation problems to the world's smartest people who compete to provide ideas and solutions to important business, social, policy, scientific, and technical challenges" (http://www.innocentive.com/about-innocentive). They provide a competitive platform and offer monetary rewards for solving challenges such as eliminating food deserts, recovering glass from demolished buildings for recycling efforts, improving mercury removal from natural gas, and increasing the affordability of inactivated poliovirus vaccine in low- and middle-income countries. These challenges address problems that currently plague the global market and need to be solved by innovative and creative individuals. However, the question remains: Are our schools properly preparing our students to solve these challenges?

Project Breaker describes its mission as a "drive [toward] social innovation and alternative learning by mobilizing interdisciplinary teams of young creative collaborators to help solve the world's most pressing problems" (http://www.projectbreaker.org/about). While their focus is on college-age students, 18–24, teachers of all grade levels can take a look at the challenges posed by Project Breaker to gain ideas and make modifications. A recent challenge tackled by Project Breaker participants included considering the role of emerging technologies to help eradicate functional illiteracy in the United States. Imagine having your students participate in a challenging investigation such as this!

Figure 2.1   Sources of Challenging Investigations

Check out these sites for ideas on challenging investigations:

- InnoCentive . . . . www.innocentive.com/ar/challenge/browse
- Project Breaker. . . . . .www.projectbreaker.org

Critical Thinking

The critical-thinking process is one that is both meaningful and necessary, but it is often overlooked in a traditional classroom. Rather than creating students who are simple consumers of information, critical thinking promotes deeper learning by students, as they become producers of information. Through critical thinking, students manipulate the researched information to produce new content. In the course of the critical-thinking process, students truly learn and understand the content, as they are able to apply it in new situations and evaluate it.

Often students become masters of memorizing content. However, many students who struggle with memorization are left believing they are "not smart" or just aren't "good at school." Introducing critical thinking at all levels calls for teachers to incorporate opportunities for predicting, modeling, forecasting, and developing the questioning process. Students are given the possibility to evaluate alternative solutions, metacognitively develop a structure for solving a problem, and continuously improve their thinking skills.

The key to the critical-thinking process is ensuring that students are appropriately challenged. A critical-thinking question that is too complex can create frustration, a sense of defeat, and ultimately abandonment of the task at hand. This is also true of the connection of the investigation to the students. Thus, teachers need to understand the makeup of their students, their needs, and their interests! What motivates your students, and how does it connect to your content? Having your students create a model of a DNA strand may be engaging for some, but asking your students to investigate possible drug combinations to create a new therapy for an existing disease is more meaningful. Ask Marshall Zhang, who in 2011 at sixteen years old worked with his mentor to do just that for cystic fibrosis (Parry, 2011). You could also talk to Angela Zhang, who in 2012 at the age of seventeen developed a potential cure for cancer ("Angela Zhang, High School Student Devises Potential Cure for Cancer," 2012). While both examples were a part of science competitions, these are the types of challenging investigations that we should provide for all our students. Modifications can be made as required to meet the needs of all learners, but the opportunity to move beyond merely replicating DNA strands should exist for all students. Save the DNA strand model replication for a scaffolding activity in the greater context of the challenging investigation.

It is entirely possible to create challenging investigations for even our lowest level IEP students. In fact, our students who are traditionally not challenged find satisfaction in being contributing members for solving these investigations. Providing the possibility for our IEP students to move beyond simple memorization of the course content opens up new avenues of understanding. In fact, with the appropriate supports, many of our IEP students are able to flourish for the first time in a school setting. Critical thinking is often an opportunity that has been traditionally denied these students in the general education classroom. However, creating Authentic Learning Experiences provides the chance to meet the diverse needs of these learners, while also appropriately challenging our honors and AP-tracked students.

Differentiation is paramount, however, and creating a challenging investigation that meets the needs of all students is necessary so that teachers don't become overly taxed and students don't believe they are being treated differently.

The Challenging Investigation

So, how do we create a challenging investigation? Ultimately, we need to start with our standards and our content. Creating a challenging investigation that is too broad might confuse students, while creating one that is too narrow will not allow us to meet our curricular demands. Finding a balance is key. Use content outlines to discover natural connections. Determine where subjects intersect to make the interdisciplinary connections that are further discussed in Chapter 7. Make real-world connections between the content and the investigation. Determine the problems with which communities, companies, and adults are faced. Let these be your starting points.

> ### ✔ Check for Understanding
> Review one of the websites listed at the start of this chapter to get ideas for a challenging investigation. Pick two or three possible ideas and link them to your course standards. Make the determination of where each topic might fit in your curriculum and what core concepts would be included in the investigation. Review this with a teaching partner or colleague.

Often teachers design a unit around a debatable topic. For example, "Is war justified?" is an age-old question that could be debated in class, addressed in a position paper, or even discussed in a simulated U.N. General Assembly meeting. Any of these activities could be successfully completed, and many students might enjoy the topic. It certainly requires more than the mere memorization of facts. However, overall, a challenging investigation should focus more on having students ultimately solve a problem or produce something that is tangible. Thus, the original debatable question could be reframed into the question posed in Chapter 1: "How can we create a plan to completely withdraw U.S. troops from Afghanistan by the end of the fiscal year?" This plan would then be presented to a group of veterans, a legislator, or, as previously noted, to a currently deployed soldier. Through their investigation, students would have to learn the causes and outcomes of past wars. However, rather than memorizing specific dates of battles or names of generals, students would be required to apply the information to support their plan for withdrawal. Battle strategies, successes and defeats, and lessons learned from each of the wars would have a place in the interconnectedness of the content and the challenging investigation. I have found this method to be a way to ground students in the task at hand. It presents the students with the goal that must be accomplished. It is also open-ended enough so that different students, groups of students, and classes will come up with quite different end answers. This is a desired outcome. In fact, this promotes the third element of Authentic Learning Experiences, justification, which is discussed in more detail in Chapter 4.

Keep in mind that the original, debatable topic could still be incorporated into the challenging investigation. It would certainly be feasible to have students complete any of the aforementioned activities as scaffolding pieces to the larger Authentic Learning Experience. It would be perfectly reasonable to plan a day to have students debate the issue or conduct the U.N. simulation. They could then use their overall thoughts on the justification of war to motivate their quest to determine a viable plan for the withdrawal of troops from Afghanistan. For example, a student who believes the conflict in Afghanistan is not justifiable could promote a plan to rapidly withdraw the troops through a system of ceasing all combat and creating a calendar of troop removal with only support services being maintained for a limited period of time. On the other hand, a student who believes the conflict in Afghanistan is justifiable could promote a steady removal of troops through a system of intense training for Afghan troops and an education program for young Afghanis.

To inspire you to create your own challenging investigations, examples of a variety of grade-level investigations that are related to several different content areas are listed in Figure 2.2 (page 18). Depending on your content focus, different subject areas may be targeted. Additionally, many of these questions could be modified in their content focus to apply to any grade level. An elementary question could be used in a high school course, but the level of investigation and content focus would be deeper. For example, the elementary question, "How can we reduce the amount of trash we produce?" could keep any K–5 student engaged, and the focus may be on both social studies and scientific concepts. Students might investigate ways that they could promote recycling in their community and the benefits of recycling. At the high school level, in an environmental science class, students might work on the development of a new method for recycling that requires less energy. Or, in a government class, students might analyze environmental legislation and write new legislation to increase recycling efforts. As you read each of the examples, remember that each of these is an open-ended, task-oriented possibility and requires students to solve a real-life problem.

Figure 2.2   Grade-Level Challenging Inquiries

GRADE LEVEL	POSSIBLE FOCUS SUBJECTS	POSSIBLE CHALLENGING INQUIRY #1	POSSIBLE CHALLENGING INQUIRY #2
Elementary school	Math, ELA, science, social studies	How can we reduce the amount of trash we produce?	How can we help the local park raise funds to build a better playground? (You could also add the math element of designing a playground here.)
Middle school	1. ELA, math, physical education 2. ELA, science	How can we create a plan to encourage more students in our school to exercise?	How can we create a plan to have our township clean the roads after a snowfall in a more efficient and environmentally friendly way?
High school	1. Law, statistics 2. Civics, ELA, statistics, science	How can we design a plan to decrease crime in our county?	How can we influence pending legislation? (This could be focused on either state or national legislative issues and based on any content area.)

Teaching Critical-Thinking Skills

Students who are younger may find challenging investigations to be less threatening than older students, who have been "traditionally educated" for a longer period of time. Learning the game of school has become second nature to many, while it has become the distraction for others. Teaching students how to think critically may be necessary. Scaffolding of information to lead to critical thinking is imperative at this stage. We can't expect our students to innately know how to think critically in the classroom without providing them with support.

Teaching critical-thinking skills must start with an exploration of Bloom's Taxonomy. Take your students through each level of Bloom's. Teach them the difference between a knowledge-level question and an application-level question. Demonstrate and model how to evaluate and apply. Ultimately push students toward the level of creation as noted in the updated version of Bloom's. Use concrete examples, such as those shown in Figure 2.3 below, to guide students through these levels of thinking so that they can grasp how to think critically. Be aware that many students may need additional support and time to process the levels. Just as we must differentiate in other areas of our teaching, we too must differentiate when it comes to teaching critical-thinking skills. This is part of the scaffolding process when introducing a challenging investigation. Thus, if this is your first foray into creating Authentic Learning Experiences, you may find you need to spend a significant amount of time on supporting students in their quest to think critically. It is, however, time well spent!

The examples listed in Figure 2.3 include questions designed to meet Common Core standard G.MG.3 ("Apply geometric methods to solve design problems") and standard 7.G.6 ("Solve real-world and mathematical problems involving area, volume and surface area of two- and three-dimensional objects composed of triangles, quadrilaterals, polygons, cubes, and right prisms"). Each of the examples could be further developed into a series of lessons that would take place throughout a challenging investigation. Note that each of the questions provides building blocks in the students' understanding and eventual goal of designing a new pool for the school.

Figure 2.3   Levels of Critical Thinking

CREATION	How can we design a new pool for our school and convince the school board to build it?
EVALUATING	How can we redesign the container using the same surface area to maximize its volume?
ANALYZING	What is the relationship between the formula for the area of a quadrilateral and surface area of a right prism?
APPLYING	Given the floor plan, how would you calculate the square footage of the house?
UNDERSTANDING	How would you compare the area of a triangle and the area of a quadrilateral?
REMEMBERING	What is the formula for the area of a rectangle?

Note: Thanks to my former colleague Hank Buckingham for inspiring this activity. It is based on an Authentic Learning Experience he conducted with his ninth-grade geometry students a few years ago when it was determined that a pool would be added to the high school. Also, thanks to my friend and math expert Telannia Norfar for making recommendations.

Figure 2.4 (below) models possible activities to be incorporated into daily scaffolding lessons that also promote the development of the critical-thinking process and can be used as formative assessments of the students' learning and skill development.

Figure 2.4 Activities for Promoting Critical-Thinking Skills

ACTIVITY	ACTIVITY EXTENSION
Have students participate in a debate in which they must argue for the side that is in opposition to their own beliefs.	■ Require students to argue from the perspective of a current political figure. ■ Younger students could argue from the viewpoint of a character instead.
Have students conduct a "silent" debate in which they write their position in a paragraph and the person next to them provides a written response. The paragraphs (virtual or hard copy) can be passed as many times as you wish.	■ Have groups of students compare and contrast the viewpoints from the silent debate, categorizing each view and possible reasons for the viewpoints. ■ Younger students could draw instead of write, and the interpretations of the drawings could lead to an interesting discussion!
Have students sequence a series of pictures related to your content. Require students to justify their sequencing process.	■ Have students tell a story about a series of seemingly unrelated pictures. The pictures should pertain to the content of your unit.

Innovation is at the heart of the challenging investigation and can be displayed in many formats. Unfortunately, there are too few opportunities for innovation in our schools today. Rather than focusing on what many perceive to be the apathetic tendencies of this generation, we must ask ourselves: How do we tap into the capabilities of this generation to promote its innate innovative spirit? Review these Authentic Learning Experiences for more ideas that draw on and support innovation. Note the promotion of the critical-thinking process, but also observe how the investigation is appropriately challenging for the students. Feel free to modify the projects as needed, and if they don't fit your curriculum, use them for the inspiring possibilities they encourage.

Sample Authentic Learning Experiences

Funding the Food Bank

Jenica Beecher
Sherwood Charter School
Sherwood, Oregon

School Background
Sherwood is a small K–8 charter school in a growing rural community. The focus of the school is to provide interdisciplinary study opportunities for student learning. This is a natural fit for the teachers at the school, as there is one teacher per elementary grade level and a team of three middle school teachers.

Challenging Investigation
How can we effectively support the local Oregon Food Bank?

Authentic Learning Experience Description
As a way to bond with her students through volunteer work and have them make direct connections with the community, Jenica Beecher decided to take her students on a field trip to the local Oregon Food Bank. At the food bank, the students repackaged oats by scooping them out of huge bins and into smaller bags. Students also received a tour of the food bank facility with an accompanying discussion on how the food bank serviced community families in need. A student spontaneously asked what they could do to help the food bank in other ways. The response, not surprisingly, was to donate money so that the food bank could purchase more food in bulk, thus obtaining more food for a lesser cost.

Upon returning from the field trip, the class read "The Little Match Girl," by Hans Christian Andersen. Following the class reading, the students engaged in a serious discussion about poverty and starvation. In fact, several students broke down in tears as Beecher reviewed current statistics about children living in poverty in the United States. A deeper discussion focused on situational poverty and the causes of it. What began as merely a field trip to the local food bank turned into a student-created experience that engaged them in designing their own challenging investigation that clearly made a community connection.

It was interesting to see the students brainstorm ideas for supporting the food bank and make the connections between their ideas and the field trip. Through the justification process, students quickly realized that a canned food drive would not be as effective as actually raising funds for the food bank. Thus, students began their quest to raise money. Over the course of the next few months, students created many different fund-raisers that ranged from selling pens to car washes. In each instance, the students had to work through the justification process as they proposed the types of fund-raisers and had to get administrative approval for each event, as well as the approval for the car-wash site and the use of the water. Students practiced their writing skills as they submitted their written requests to the appropriate persons.

Students integrated the math component of their project throughout the fund-raising efforts. They had to count money, make cost projections, and determine profits. Ultimately, the students presented the Oregon Food Bank with $500 in raised money. Students wrote letters regarding their learning to an outside audience, the food bank officials.

COMMON CORE STATE STANDARDS

3.RL.1	Ask and answer questions to demonstrate understanding of a text, referring explicitly to the text as the basis for the answers.
3.RL.3	Describe characters in a story and explain how their actions contribute to the sequence of events.
3.RL.6	Distinguish their own point of view from that of the narrator or those of the characters.
3.W.1	Write opinion pieces on topics or texts, supporting a point of view with reasons.
3.W.2	Write informative/expository texts to examine a topic and convey ideas and information clearly.
3.W.4	With guidance and support from adults, produce writing in which the development and organization are appropriate to task and purpose.
3.W.5	With guidance and support from peers and adults, develop and strengthen writing as needed by planning, revising, and editing.
3.L.3	Use knowledge of language and its conventions when writing, speaking, reading, or listening.
3.L.5	Demonstrate understanding of figurative language, word relationships and nuances in word meanings.
3.OA.2	Interpret whole-number quotients of whole numbers.

3.NBT.1	Use place value understanding to round whole numbers to the nearest 10 or 100.
3.NF.3	Explain equivalence of fractions in special cases, and compare fractions by reasoning about their size.
3.MD.2	Measure and estimate liquid volumes and masses of objects using standard units of grams, kilograms, and liters. Add, subtract, multiply, or divide to solve one-step word problems involving masses or volumes that are given in the same units.

Technology Integration

At the time this experience was implemented, technology was scarce in the school. However, the students were able to successfully participate in the experience without integrating technology. If technology were to be added to a similar experience, there would be room for the use of many collaborative tools such as Google Docs or for the use of Glogster to create posters to advertise for the fund-raisers.

Teacher Reflection

"Our charter school used to require us to plan one field trip per month. Most of the field trips go along with our core knowledge units, while others are for helping the students develop as community members. I decided to take my third-grade students to the Oregon Food Bank to do some volunteer work as a way of bonding with each other and helping other community members. When we returned to the classroom and read 'The Little Match Girl,' a required reading for our core content knowledge, somehow this turned into a 'What can we do about this?' conversation. So the students launched a yearlong campaign to raise money for the Oregon Food Bank.

"The kids felt wonderful about their accomplishment, even if they didn't meet their goal of $1,000. Sadly, though, we never heard back from the Oregon Food Bank. If I were to do this again, I would have the students present the check in person instead of sending it through the mail."—Jenica Beecher

iGreenCR

Ryan Rydstrom
Prairie Point Middle School and Ninth Grade Academy
Cedar Rapids, Iowa

School Background
This public school serves approximately 1,100 seventh- through ninth-grade students in the College Community School District in Cedar Rapids, Iowa. The district is a suburban community that also exhibits many aspects of a rural district. The purpose of the ninth-grade academy is to create a smaller learning community for students in order to help them make a smoother transition into the high school the following year.

Challenging Investigation
How can Cedar Rapids become a more sustainable community?

Authentic Learning Experience Description
Ninth-grade physical science students' study of the law of conservation of mass in relation to Earth's natural cycles and the assessment of the effects of human consumption on these cycles led them to an exploration of the challenging investigation. Students used their understanding of these topics to go deeper into the content and standards of how to apply scientific evidence to analyze cause and effect. Students interviewed a variety of city officials as they worked in collaborative groups to calculate carbon emissions and carbon savings. Their additional focus on chemical formulas and reactions of elements propelled them to make informed decisions in order to focus on the need for justification for their proposals on how to set goals for ways in which the city could effectively reduce its carbon footprint. Since the focus was on the city in which the students reside, the community connection was readily apparent, and the significance for the students in completing this Authentic Learning Experience was evident. As the students navigated through the process of analyzing data, applying scientific concepts, and conducting a cost-benefit investigation, they worked toward the ultimate goal of presenting their solutions to the challenging investigation to a panel of experts. This outside audience included members of the Cedar Rapids City

Council, local college professors, and school district administrators. In addition to the presentation, students had to submit a formal written report that included an abstract, a definition of the problem, the analysis of the data, and the implications of the proposed solution.

COMMON CORE STATE STANDARDS

9.RIT.1	Cite strong and thorough textual evidence to support analysis of what the text says explicitly as well as inferences drawn from the text.
9.RIT.2	Determine a central idea of a text and analyze its development over the course of the text, including how it emerges and is shaped and refined by specific details; provide an objective summary of the text.
9.W.1	Write arguments to support claims in an analysis of substantive topics or texts, using valid reasoning and relevant and sufficient evidence.
9.W.7	Conduct short as well as more sustained research projects to answer a question (including a self-generated question) or solve a problem; narrow or broaden the inquiry when appropriate; synthesize multiple sources on the subject, demonstrating understanding of the subject under investigation.
9.SL.4	Present information, findings, and supporting evidence clearly, concisely, and logically such that listeners can follow the line of reasoning and the organization, development, substance, and style are appropriate to purpose, audience, and task.
N.Q.1	Use units as a way to understand problems and to guide the solution of multi-step problems; choose and interpret units consistently in formulas; choose and interpret the scale and the origin in graphs and data displays.
N.Q.3	Choose a level of accuracy appropriate to limitations on measurement when reporting quantities.
S.ID.2	Use statistics appropriate to the shape of the data distribution to compare center and spread of two or more different data sets.
S.ID.3	Interpret differences in shape, center, and spread in the context of the data sets, accounting for possible effects of extreme data points.
G.MG.3	Apply geometric methods to solve design problems.
S.MD.7	Analyze decisions and strategies using probability concepts.

Technology Integration

Students used Google Apps and Google Docs to collaborate on their work.

Teacher Reflection

"'When will I ever use this stuff? I am not going to be a scientist!' During my first year of teaching, this was a typical comment from my students. Of course, I could answer the question with various examples. However, that just didn't cut it for my students. They needed to DO it. They need to EXPERIENCE it. They needed to LIVE it. They needed to become SCIENTISTS.

"I was determined to give my students what they needed. A consultant from Cedar Rapids Utilities Department was looking for a teacher to collaborate with on educating the community on new sustainable initiatives in Cedar Rapids. I finally had my connection. The iGreenCR project is a manifestation of this collaboration.

"My expectations of my students increased exponentially once I started implementing this project. My teaching was no longer dictated by superficial unit outlines and end-of-unit tests. The students had to apply and explain all the standards and concepts in a real-world context. They had to present their findings, write a report, and answer questions from experts. I'm not saying I didn't have a rigorous curriculum to begin with, but this experience stepped it up a notch. The students had to make adult decisions that could affect the community. They were finally doing it, experiencing it, and living it. They were finally scientists, and they finally saw when they would use this 'stuff' in their lives."—Ryan Rydstrom

A Question of Native American Affairs

Andrew Miller
Technology Access Foundation Academy of Federal Way Public Schools
Kent, Washington

School Background

The TAF Academy is a school of choice within the Federal Way Public Schools. Choice schools in Washington are typically housed within an existing larger school but have a designated curricular focus. The focus at TAF is on a STEM curriculum with the goal to provide students the opportunity to become active participants in their own education.

Challenging Investigation

How can we help our senator make the best decisions for Native Americans in Washington State?

Authentic Learning Experience Description

In his first real foray into creating an Authentic Learning Experience for his students, Andrew Miller had his humanities class focus on an issue that is constantly a source of debate in the state of Washington. As the Native American tribal governments have found a way to be economically profitable through the creation of casinos on reservations, they have also created jobs, tourism, and increased revenue for the state at large. However, these tribal government actions have had an impact on the social, economic, and fiscal decisions of the Washington state government. Additionally, the state government has historically provided limited funding for the tribal populations. Thus, the community connection to the challenging investigation was explored in an effort to brief Senator Maria Cantwell, who serves on the Committee of Indian Affairs, on ways in which her committee could positively impact the Native Americans in Washington State.

The students conducted research and completed data analyses of the impact of the casinos on the cultures of the tribes. As a part of the humanities curriculum, the students also explored the changing historical plight of the Native Americans within their state. The focus of the assessment of the students' learning was to write a persuasive piece, as well as complete a presentation to Cantwell's legislative director, on the next steps for the legislature to positively impact Native American affairs. However, students also completed a written informational briefing that focused on the depth of content knowledge gained throughout the four-week experience. Both the persuasive piece and the oral presentation to the senator's legislative director provided students with an outside audience, for which each portion of the proposal required a justification of their recommendations.

COMMON CORE STATE STANDARDS

9.RIT.1	Cite strong and thorough textual evidence to support analysis of what the text says explicitly as well as inferences drawn from the text.
9.RIT.8	Delineate and evaluate the argument and specific claims in a text, assessing whether the reasoning is valid and the evidence is relevant and sufficient; identify false statements and fallacious reasoning.
9.W.1	Write arguments to support claims in an analysis of substantive topics or texts, using valid reasoning and relevant and sufficient evidence.
9.W.4	Produce clear and coherent writing in which the development, organization, and style are appropriate to task, purpose, and audience.
9.W.5	Develop and strengthen writing as needed by planning, revising, editing, rewriting, or trying a new approach, focusing on addressing what is most significant for a specific purpose and audience.
9.W.7	Conduct short as well as more sustained research projects to answer a question (including a self-generated question) or solve a problem; narrow or broaden the inquiry when appropriate; synthesize multiple sources on the subject, demonstrating understanding of the subject under investigation.
9.W.9	Draw evidence from literary or informational texts to support analysis, reflection, and research.
9.SL.4	Present information, findings, and supporting evidence clearly, concisely, and logically so that listeners can follow the line of reasoning and the organization, development, substance, and style are appropriate to purpose, audience, and task.

Technology Integration

The one-to-one technology program allowed students to enhance their collaboration on this project through the use of the district's learning management system.

Teacher Reflection

"Looking back on the project, I would like to modify the products students completed to allow for more choice. I had many formative assessments to evaluate students individually on content, but no large one. Instead of an informational briefing, I would fold that information and content into the presentation and have students do a persuasive writing of their choice, rather than a teacher-directed one, including a letter or editorial to actually send to the appropriate audience. In terms of the authenticity of this experience, when students knew the information was REALLY going to their audience, the senator, and that the audience would respond, it made the project more challenging and created more of a buy-in to complete it. This was the best part of the overall project design."—Andrew Miller

CHAPTER 3

— ■ —

Creating the Community/Career Connection

Historically, it has been necessary that our schools and teachers create an educated student who is prepared both to enter the competitive workforce and to be socially responsible. Although we live in an era of standardized educational testing, it is imperative that educational opportunities for the development of these skills still exist. Creating an Authentic Learning Experience that supports either a direct connection to a potential career for students or creates a social contract for students to enter is paramount. This doesn't mean that we walk away from preparing students for state testing or discourage them from taking Advanced Placement courses that require testing. In fact, a carefully crafted Authentic Learning Experience will create a well-rounded student who is prepared to meet the demands of testing from all avenues.

Career Connection
While it is widely known that not all students will walk into our classrooms with a predetermined career path and it is predicted that many careers our students may one day choose have yet to be created, students must still be exposed to a wide variety of options. Sparking career interest in young stu-

dents can have an impact that promotes additional career preparation in future years, thus helping to motivate and guide them. (How many of you knew you wanted to be a teacher at a very young age?) Therefore, one option in creating an Authentic Learning Experience can focus on making a tie to a particular career or careers. However, it should be noted that this type of Authentic Learning Experience should not be reserved only for career academy schools, career technical education schools, or magnet and charter schools that have a predetermined career focus. We need to move away from designing experiences that limit the opportunities that students have to think critically or to truly engage in an open-ended challenging investigation. All students deserve the opportunity to be engaged in career development and even more so as the Common Core State Standards are implemented in order to create a focus on "career and college readiness." Rather than giving students the plans to build a house, it is time to give students the opportunity to help design that house and build it. Students at Hana High and Elementary in Hana, Hawaii, participate in similar experiences. They have crafted a skate park for the community, built a solar shower for a family in need, and built an alternative energy lab for the school, just to name a few experiences.

When it is appropriate in the curriculum, create opportunities to align with a career focus. Determine what areas of your curriculum naturally lead to a career connection. Ask yourself: Are these tasks in which professionals in my curricular area would engage? For instance, in my own law classroom, I have students participate in a mock crime scene in which they take on the roles of crime scene investigators, police officers, forensic psychologists, lawyers, and judges, among others. Students are able to make their top three choices for a potential role and stay in character for the duration of the three-week experience, which culminates in a mock trial that is presented in front of a jury that includes experts. A colleague of mine, chemistry teacher Matt Williams, has had his students take on the role of chemists as they create chemical compounds for new cleaning solutions that are both cost- and performance-effective. These solutions are then pitched to the custodial staff at our school. Figure 3.1 (page 33) offers additional ideas for making connections with experts in a field.

In career-connection cases, we know that most students involved in the Authentic Learning Experience will not select the careers to which they have been exposed. However, if we have sparked interest in some and others have learned they are *not* interested in certain careers, we have succeeded. Check out the ideas in Figure 3.2 (page 33) for ways to make a career connection in your own classroom.

Figure 3.1   Ideas for Making Connections with Experts

- Talk to your district's career counselor.
- Send an e-mail to your colleagues to ask if they have any relatives or friends who are experts in the area in which you are searching.
- Post a request in your school's newsletter or on the school website asking for parents who are experts in the field to volunteer their time.
- Make a cold call—you might be surprised!

Figure 3.2   Ideas for Making Career Connections in the Classroom

CONTENT AREA	CAREER CONNECTION	CHALLENGING INVESTIGATION
Social studies	Historian	How can we create a series of oral histories of prominent members of our community to be recorded for the local historical society?
Science	Soil scientist	How can we cost-effectively improve soil conditions around our school and on the sports field to make the grass look greener?
Math	Urban planner	How can we design improvements to our city/town to revitalize the area and attract new businesses?
ELA	Poet	How can we create a coffeehouse poetry reading for the community?
Art	Gallery curator, sculptor, painter	How can we design an art gallery exhibit to showcase the history of our community?
Foreign language	Interpreter	How can we bridge the gap for ELL students who speak the language we are studying?* * For upper-level language classes
Physical education	Athletic trainer	How can we create an engaging workout plan designed to increase physical activity in our school that students will stick to?
Music, drama	Songwriter, composer, producer, playwright	How can we create an original musical score and dramatic production that teaches a lesson?
Culinary arts, business, graphic design	Chef, accountant, advertising manager	How can we run a successful and profitable restaurant for our school?

Community Connection

When creating an Authentic Learning Experience that focuses on a community connection, you first need to determine at which level of the community you would like to engage. Community connections can be made at the school level, the local level, the state level, the national level, and even the global level. It may be advisable to start at the school or local level until you become comfortable with the process and make the appropriate connections on a larger scale. In any case, making these community connections is imperative so that we encourage students to gain a respect for and an understanding of social responsibility.

Creating a context to promote the understanding of a social contract should not be reserved for the social studies classroom. This agreement among members of a society to work toward the greater good of that society should be practiced on all levels. In fact, most social studies classrooms merely study the concept of the social contract and rarely put it into practice. Thus, it is necessary to move beyond civic engagement as a notion that is reserved for the adult population and engage all students and all classes in the quest for societal improvements.

It is also important to connect our schools to the communities where they are located. Creating Authentic Learning Experiences that connect the students to local community elements can do wonders for the relationship between the school district and the members of the community. There has been a notable lack of understanding between the community at large and the districts that they support. Using an Authentic Learning Experience to bridge the gap between the two can help to dispel common misconceptions and misunderstandings between the two entities.

> ### ☑ Check for Understanding
> Read a local or national newspaper or newsmagazine of your choice. Pick the top three headlines from the day, and determine where in your content they might fit. Develop a challenging investigation that fits the headline. Review your design with a teaching partner or colleague.

The challenging investigation could be linked directly to the school community, could involve a local community problem, or could focus on a pressing national or foreign issue. The community/career connection increases student motivation for learning. No longer is the material simply something to be memorized from a textbook, but it is relevant and engaging for the students. This element takes away the "Why do I need to know this?" question. This element is also strongly tied to the 21st-century skill of collaboration, as it is necessary for students to work collectively to explore the challenging investigation. Take a look at the examples in Figure 3.3 (below) for connections between the community and the challenging investigation.

> *"I wanted to again thank you both for the opportunity to observe your class presentation on crime. We often only see and hear the bad that society has to offer, but it's times such as this that we get to appreciate the good that our young people are involved in."*
> —a representative of a district attorney's office in reference to a presentation by students in a co-taught inclusion classroom

Figure 3.3   Community Connections to the Challenging Investigation

COMMUNITY CONTEXT	POSSIBLE CHALLENGING INVESTIGATION
School	How can we increase the number of active readers in our school?
Local	How can we reduce the number of traffic accidents that occur in our county?
State	How can we gain the most benefits from the extraction of natural gas that is occurring in our state, but promote a plan to reduce the negative environmental effects of the process?
National	How can we, as a society, become less reliant on petroleum from foreign nations?
Global	How can we create a plan for U.S. involvement to promote peace between the Israelis and Palestinians?

Note: Each challenging investigation could be presented in a multitude of ways to a variety of experts, depending on your goals for the Authentic Learning Experience.

Students crave opportunities to get involved in their communities. There are countless young people from all over the globe who are already taking their own initiative to give back to others. Can you imagine the potential to link these opportunities to not only social responsibility and the learning that automatically takes place with it but also the connection between the academic world and the social contract that our youth deserve to experience? See the information in Figure 3.4 (page 36) to explore ways in which students are already giving back and for inspiration for creating an Authentic Learning Experience for your own classroom that connects the community aspect to your content. The influence of the involvement of one student can translate into a powerful experience between many students who are giving and those who are receiving.

Taking students on the journey through a challenging investigation that has a community or career connection can be a rewarding experience for both the students and the teacher. Not only does academic learning take place, but social and personal transformation can also take place. Take a look at these Authentic Learning Experience examples that make either the community or career connection, and make it your goal to do the same.

Figure 3.4   Examples of Young People Engaging in Social Responsibility

- Kids Are Heroes. . . . . www.kidsareheroes.org
- Kids Making a Difference . . . . www.kmad.org
- Kids Can Make a Difference (iEARN) . . . . .www.kidscanmakeadifference.org

Career Connection Examples

Pinball Wizard

Ross Cooper
Willow Lane Elementary
Macungie, Pennsylvania

School Background

Willow Lane is a STEM-focused public school that serves grades K–5 and is one of seven elementary schools in the East Penn School District. The school is located in the rural community of Macungie, Pennsylvania, a suburb of Allentown. The mission statement for the school district promotes the integration of Authentic Learning Experiences through providing "a learning environment in which students become problem solvers, collaborators, and critical thinkers."

Challenging Investigation

How can we apply engineering concepts to create our own pinball machines?

Authentic Learning Experience Description

It is never too early to teach students engineering concepts, and what better way to do so than to use pinball machines? In this Authentic Learning Experience, students made a career connection to the engineering world as they created their own pinball machines. The content students learned from this project included a great deal of engineering concepts that are used by professional engineers. The curricular concepts included the study of electrical circuits and all their components, magnets, electromagnets, Newton's laws of motion, force, gravity, friction, and mathematical concepts of measurement and geometry.

A lot of scaffolding work took place during this lengthy experience, as students had to include flippers, bumpers, launchers, and a working electrical circuit on their machines. In order to ensure that the fourth-grade students weren't too overwhelmed, each component of the experience had to be broken down into smaller chunks. Throughout the process, students created a pre-blueprint, a blueprint, and finally a working pinball machine. To help increase their understanding of force and motion, as well as electricity and magnetism, the students blogged about the experiments that were part of the scaffolding process. Additional formative assessments were incorporated as each phase of the experience provided students with opportunities for feedback from both the teacher and volunteer engineers who came to the class three times. These volunteer engineers also provided students with the outside audience they needed at the conclusion of the experience. During the presentation of learning, students had to include the justification for designing their pinball machine in the manner in which they did. This, however, was easy for the students, as they ran simulations at various points of the experience to ensure the machines were strong and forceful. In the end, students certainly were able to connect their learning to the challenging investigation as they completed three summative assessments that focused on electricity and magnetism, force and motion, and the actual building of the pinball machine.

COMMON CORE STATE STANDARDS

4.W.2	Write informative/explanatory texts to examine a topic and convey ideas and information clearly.
4.W.4	Produce clear and coherent writing in which the development and organization are appropriate to task, purpose, and audience.
4.SL.1	Engage effectively in a range of collaborative discussions with diverse partners on grade 4 topics and texts, building on others' ideas and expressing their own clearly.
4.SL.4	Report on a topic or text, tell a story, or recount an experience in an organized manner, using appropriate facts and relevant, descriptive details to support main ideas or themes; speak clearly at an understandable pace.
4.MD.1	Know relative sizes of measurement units within one system of units.
4.MD.2	Use the four operations to solve word problems involving distances, intervals of time, liquid volumes, masses of objects, and money, including problems involving simple fractions or decimals, and problems that require expressing measurements given in a larger unit in terms of a smaller unit. Represent measurement quantities using diagrams such as number line diagrams that feature a measurement scale.
4.MD.5	Recognize angles as geometric shapes that are formed wherever two rays share a common endpoint, and understand concepts of angle measurement.
4.MD.6	Measure angles in whole-number degrees using a protractor. Sketch angles of specified measure.
4.G.1	Draw points, lines, line segments, rays, angles, and perpendicular and parallel lines. Identify these in two-dimensional figures.

4.G.2	Classify two-dimensional figures based on the presence or absence of parallel or perpendicular lines, or the presence or absence of angles of a specified size. Recognize right triangles as a category, and identify right triangles.

Technology Integration

Students used Moodle and Blogger to record their reflections following each of the experiments and test runs on the pinball machines. During the building phases, students employed iPod touches, iPads, iPhoto, and iMovie to help document the engineering process. Students also uploaded photos of the stages of the building to Picasa and on the classroom website in order to stay apprised of the progress of each pinball machine.

Teacher Reflection

"As the content standards were significant in this experience, the students were able to delve deeper into the content, as they were constantly engaged in problem solving, collaboration, and critical thinking. There were countless decisions that they had to make during the building of their pinball machines and as they used multiple forms of technology. Throughout the experience, the directions supplied the students with a skeleton of what they had to do, but other than that, the students completely defined the learning process. Furthermore, as students continuously wrote, researched, and reflected individually and collaboratively, they had to make changes when necessary. As a result, the student learning experience was entirely authentic, as it strongly resembles how design professionals work on a regular basis. This project has helped our school to connect with the community, as many parents and experts came in to help with the technology, to assist with the machines, or to just watch in awe as the students did their work. It is an experience that I continue to implement and refine as I watch the students grow in their knowledge and understanding of engineering principles and their applications."

—Ross Cooper

Books of Hope

Laura Bradley, National Board Certified Teacher
Kenilworth Junior High School
Petaluma, California

School Background
The Petaluma City Elementary and Joint Union High School Districts provide services to approximately 7,500 students, nearly one-quarter of whom are classified as ELLs. The Kenilworth Junior High supports 1,000 students in seventh and eighth grade. The school's mission statement includes a focus on the "recognition of each student's individual talents and abilities."

Challenging Investigation
How can we support the improvement of literacy in Ugandan children through stories we write?

Authentic Learning Experience Description
Laura Bradley has a passion for writing. That passion is contagious and has infected the students she teaches. Most writing in her eighth-grade English classes is aimed at an outside audience. Her students are truly engaged as real writers in a clear career connection to the work they produce. In fact, it's not unusual for students streaming into her classroom to ask, "Can we work on our stories today, Mrs. Bradley?" This Authentic Learning Experience was no exception, as students teamed up with Books of Hope (now E-luminate) to publish and send stories to children in Uganda. (Note: Books of Hope was initially focused on fiction stories, and E-luminate focuses on nonfiction contributions.)

Students made a global community connection through the writing process as they reached halfway around the world to an outside audience. Viewing *Invisible Children,* a documentary that chronicles the lives of those who have escaped rebel armies or spent their young lives avoiding capture by them, opened the students' eyes to the poverty-stricken living conditions and lack of educational opportunity available to Ugandan children. Thus, the challenging investigation brought meaning to their writing as they crafted their original stories. Bradley's students gained perspective into the lives of their audience as they were cautioned to omit references to material wealth and violence. Students learned to write stories that were appropriate for children ages nine through twelve and suitable for children just learning their ABCs as well. In short, stories had to be age appropriate as well as appropriate to the beginning reading level of the audience. Student writers took their story ideas through a justification process to meet the needs of their readers, and worked tirelessly proofreading, peer editing, and revising to ensure that stories would have both meaning and value to enhance the reading abilities of the Ugandan schoolchildren. The published books, which were also illustrated by Bradley's students, were bound and shipped to their new home. To add still more of the human touch, many of the young authors included their own personal photographs.

Ultimately, students realized the challenging investigation was more difficult than they initially understood. When the shipment of books arrived in Uganda, the package was not opened until all the students and teachers could be present to inventory the contents. The value of those books was far beyond what the California students could have imagined. Books like these are often confiscated by outlaws and sold on the streets for profit. The Ugandan government provides so little for the children that these simple books and a basic education were far more valuable than Bradley's students had ever realized. The lessons learned by Bradley's students through completion of this challenging investigation go far beyond the standards, far beyond grammar and composition lessons. The lessons learned, in the words of Bradley, were really about the "power of the written word."

COMMON CORE STATE STANDARDS

8.RIT.7	Evaluate the advantages and disadvantages of using different mediums (e.g., print or digital text, video, multimedia) to present a particular topic or idea.
8.W.3	Write narratives to develop real or imagined experiences or events using effective technique, relevant descriptive details, and well-structured event sequences.
8.W.4	Produce clear and coherent writing in which the development, organization, and style are appropriate to task, purpose, and audience.
8.W.5	With some guidance and support from peers and adults, develop and strengthen writing as needed by planning, revising, editing, rewriting, or trying a new approach, focusing on how well purpose and audience have been addressed.
8.W.6	Use technology, including the Internet, to produce and publish writing and present the relationships between information and ideas efficiently as well as to interact and collaborate with others.

8.W.10	Write routinely over extended time frames and shorter time frames.
8.L.1	Demonstrate command of the conventions of standard English grammar and usage when writing or speaking.
8.L.3	Use knowledge of language and its conventions when writing, speaking, reading, or listening.

Technology Integration

Books of Hope requested that the students produce books that were clearly legible and professional looking, since the books would be used in schools for academic purposes. For this reason, the students used classroom laptops to publish their stories. They learned how to format Microsoft Word documents so that their books looked as much like "real" books as possible. They learned to insert and format copyright-free images, format text, and design consistent and visually appealing layouts, as well as photograph images to illustrate their stories, which they then uploaded and inserted into their books. In addition to developing their creative writing skills, this project taught them a host of word processing, illustrating, and formatting skills.

Teacher Reflection

"The roller-coaster ride of emotions so often found in a middle school classroom can be attributed to the great depth of feelings experienced by students at this age. If they are sad, they are often deeply depressed; when they are happy, they bounce off the walls with 'anything is possible' buoyancy. If we can tap into these deep feelings to inspire them to write for a genuine audience, we often see them produce their best work. When I share the tragic stories of the Ugandan children with my eighth-grade students, their responses are heartfelt and urgent. They shed tears over the lost childhoods; they marshal resources to make a difference. And this is why the Books of Hope project inspired such enthusiastic and quality writing in my students. They saw a direct connection between a significant challenge in their world and their own writing. They were empowered to make a very real and necessary difference, and they poured their best efforts into their work, not for a grade, but for an audience they deemed worthy of quality stories. No longer seeing a disconnect between writing assignments and their lives ('Why do we have to learn this?'), my students left junior high with a clear sense of the power of the written word and their own power to improve the lives of others, even those halfway around the world."—Laura Bradley, NBCT

Geospatial Semester

Ryan Miller
Washington-Lee High School
Arlington, Virginia

School Background
Named one of the country's best high schools by *Newsweek*, Washington-Lee is
a suburban public high school located just outside of Washington, D.C. It relies
heavily on parental involvement and partnerships with community leaders and
businesses. Due to its close proximity to Washington, it is home to students from
more than fifty countries and capitalizes on their cultural diversity.

Challenging Investigation
How can we apply geographic information systems (GIS) to work on and complete
real government GIS projects that are low priority but are due for investigation and
completion by various government agencies?

Authentic Learning Experience Description
Ryan Miller's year-end projects incorporated all the GIS skills and information
gained by his students throughout the duration of his course. He had students
apply these skills and information to tackle real-world situations and scenarios that
required GIS analysis. Unfortunately, he was disappointed that the end products
were lacking in inspiration and, in truth, were overwhelming for students. The
wide-open nature of choosing a topic caused students to spend more time trying
to figure out what they wanted to focus on rather than actually applying their GIS
knowledge to the self-identified real-world problem. The faculty at JMU found
entering freshmen weren't prepared for a college workload and expectations after
spending the latter half of their senior year "slacking off" once college acceptance
letters were received. In response to this, JMU professors Bob Kolvoord and
Kathryn Keranen created the JMU Geospatial Semester. According to the JMU
description of the course, "A key aspect of the program is a focus on local projects
connecting students, technology, and their community," providing the community/
career connection necessary in an Authentic Learning Experience. In fact, this
experience provided both a community *and* a career connection!

As an incentive, students who joined Miller's senior GIS elective received JMU college credit. However, once enrolled in the course, students quickly realized they would gain more than college credit as they learned about the challenging investigation. Students ultimately picked a problem from a list of ten to fifteen uncompleted GIS projects linked with a corresponding government agency. Since government agencies are asked to provide community outreach, the agencies on whose plans these students worked were certainly happy to provide the project ideas. These agencies also ultimately provided the outside audience to whom the students presented their GIS work and solutions.

Investigations that students tackled ranged in topics from how the Metro, the area's public transportation system, affects urban development and the environment to how the U.S. Fish and Wildlife Service could automate the infrared processing of detection of government easements in wetland areas. In each instance, students were able to bring math to life, as their work became a visual representation of the problems they were investigating. As noted, students presented their findings and the justification of their conclusions to the appropriate government agency, but the outside audience extended beyond these experts. Several students were given the opportunity to travel to California to present their findings at the 2012 Esri International User Conference to nearly 15,000 audience members. In fact, the work of the students was noted as being comparable to that of the GIS professionals in attendance at the conference.

COMMON CORE STATE STANDARDS

12.RIT.4	Determine the meaning of words and phrases as they are used in a text, including figurative, connotative, and technical meanings; analyze how an author uses and refines the meaning of a key term or terms over the course of a text.
12.W.10	Write routinely over extended time frames (time for research, reflection, and revision) and shorter time frames for a range of tasks and purposes.
12.SL.2	Integrate multiple sources of information presented in diverse formats and media (e.g., visually, quantitatively, orally) in order to make informed decisions and solve problems, evaluating the credibility and accuracy of each source and noting any discrepancies among the data.
12.SL.4	Present information, findings, and supporting evidence, conveying a clear and distinct perspective, such that listeners can follow the line of reasoning, alternative or opposing perspectives are addressed, and the organization, development, substance, and style are appropriate to purpose, audience, and a range of formal and informal tasks.

12.SL.5	Make strategic use of digital media in presentations to enhance understanding of findings, reasoning, and evidence, and to add interest.
S.CP.2	Understand that two events A and B are independent if the probability of A and B occurring together is the product of their probabilities, and use this characterization to determine if they are independent.
G.MG.3	Apply geometric methods to solve design problems (e.g., designing an object or structure to satisfy physical constraints or minimize cost; working with typographic grid systems based on ratios).
S.MD.1	Define a random variable for a quantity of interest by assigning a numerical value to each event in a sample space; graph the corresponding probability distribution using the same graphical displays as for data distributions.
S.MD.2	Calculate the expected value of a random variable; interpret it as the mean of the probability distribution.

Technology Integration

The entire course is based on geographic information systems. As noted by Esri, a GIS company, GIS integrates hardware, software, and data for capturing, managing, analyzing, and displaying all forms of geographically referenced information (www.esri.com/what-is-gis).

Teacher Reflection

"I found that all students, when given the opportunity to work on and complete actual work, were completely engaged and motivated during the entirety of this experience. Urgency and thoroughness were common attributes in all of the students as they looked to apply their GIS knowledge in tackling a real problem. Every student rose to the occasion and took pride in using their abilities for the benefit of providing true assistance to the government agencies that tasked them with work. Relevance was an overarching theme to this project, as it pushed these students to be analytical in thought and practice."—Ryan Miller

Community Connection Examples

Touring Saint Louis, Kid Style

Jeff Horwitz, Amy Lamb, and Kristen Kaiser
Mary Institute and Saint Louis Country Day School
Saint Louis, Missouri

School Background

MICDS is a private, independent college preparatory K–12 school. The school represents forty different languages, as it includes a wide range of cultural diversity. The mission statement of the school reflects a desire to prepare students for collegiate enrollment, as well as to "meet the challenges of this world."

Challenging Investigation

How can we create a daylong tour of Saint Louis that is entertaining, informative, and creative, and appeals to kids visiting our city?

Authentic Learning Experience Description

Students were asked by the St. Louis Convention & Visitors Commission to ponder what made Saint Louis special. The challenging investigation grew out of this initial question and had an obvious community connection. Students were placed in small groups and tasked with researching potential tourist sites in Saint Louis to determine the best fit for an "ultimate" tour. Students, who were also given a $200 budget for tour-planning purposes, had to choose their destination sites carefully. Not only did students have to go through the justification process to validate the inclusion of the sites they suggested, which was based on the appeal to potential visitors, but they also had to meet the constraints of their budget. To promote additional critical thinking, as well as to help convince the commission to include the site, students had to create an activity to accompany the tour stop. Additionally, students were required to write a persuasive paragraph about the justification for their tourist destination.

Students eventually presented their proposals using a variety of creative approaches that included developing commercials to sell their ideas to the Visitors Commission, who were the perfect outside audience for this experience. The Visitors Commission then took the ideas from the nine small-group presentations to formally develop a kid-friendly tour for Saint Louis. This tour can be viewed on the Explore St. Louis website (www.explorestlouis.com). At the conclusion of the Authentic Learning Experience, the students were afforded the opportunity to take this tour and realize how their work translated into the real world.

COMMON CORE STATE STANDARDS

2.RIT.1	Ask and answer such questions as *who, what, where, when, why,* and *how* to demonstrate understanding of key details in a text.
2.RIT.4	Determine the meaning of words and phrases in a text relevant to a grade 2 topic or subject area.
2.RIT.6	Identify the main purpose of a text, including what the author wants to answer, explain, or describe.
2.W.1	Write opinion pieces in which they introduce the topic or book they are writing about, state an opinion, supply reasons that support the opinion, use linking words to connect opinion and reasons, and provide a concluding statement or section.
2.W.2	Write informative/explanatory texts in which they introduce a topic, use facts and definitions to develop points, and provide a concluding statement or section.
2.W.5	With guidance and support from adults and peers, focus on a topic and strengthen writing as needed by revising and editing.
2.W.6	With guidance and support from adults, use a variety of digital tools to produce and publish writing, including in collaboration with peers.
2.W.7	Participate in shared research and writing projects.
2.SL.1	Participate in collaborative conversations with diverse partners about grade 2 topics and texts with peers and adults in small and large groups.
2.L.1	Demonstrate command of the conventions of standard English grammar and usage when writing or speaking.

Technology Integration

Technology was an integral tool to help students achieve their end goal for this experience. All students used the Internet to research their landmark through the landmark's website. Once their research was complete, students used many different technology tools to create their unique and informative products. These tools ranged from iPhoto and iMovie, to create a commercial for the presentation of their site, to Microsoft Word, to type their paragraphs.

Teacher Reflection

"This experience was successful because the students were engaged and motivated by the introduction to the task. They immediately knew what they were trying to achieve and were excited to have their work featured on the Explore St. Louis website. An added motivation was the fact that their work would actually be used as the class went on the tour of Saint Louis. Students gained so much respect for this project. They gained content knowledge of what a landmark is and information about many of the landmarks in their community. They gained research, teamwork, collaboration, communication, critical-thinking, and presentation skills. By connecting the students with the community, it made the experience authentic and meaningful. It also freed the teachers up from being fountains of knowledge and the evaluators of the work to become the architects of opportunity for the students."—Jeff Horwitz

Trash2Art

Sabine LeDieu and Michelle Sears
Springfield Middle School
Battle Creek, Michigan

School Background

Springfield Middle School is an urban middle school (grades 5–8) in the Springfield, Michigan, area. Springfield is a suburb of the larger city of Battle Creek, Michigan. The district services a very diverse population.

Challenging Investigation

How can we create art that promotes environmental stewardship in the community?

Authentic Learning Experience Description

The ETC ARTS Studio, a nonprofit organization, teamed up with classes ranging from elementary school to high school to explore environmental issues in art. The ETC ARTS Studio actually created this Authentic Learning Experience for students based on its own challenging investigation: "How do you reach the next generation with art?" Backed with funding from Calhoun County Solid Waste Department, the studio tapped into the "reduce, reuse, and recycle" motto to work with five different schools from the county. Each school's project took a different focus, but Springfield Middle School students created their art for installation in the community at the farmers' market. These students' answer to the challenging investigation "How can we create art that promotes environmental stewardship in the community?" was to create a bottle-cap sculpture of the words "LOVE RECYCLING." The unveiling of the art on Earth Day 2012 was the ultimate example of an outside audience; students gave speeches about the program and their sculpture. In these speeches, students noted their justification for their final sculpture and worked to persuade attendees to get more involved in recycling.

During the course of the project, students first worked to create sculptures in class in preparation for work in the real studio. The students then received six workshop experiences. Many of the students also came to the studio in their free time and utilized peer-to-peer text messaging during the project in order to share information.

Furthering the community connection, students and local businesses collected metal and plastic bottle tops for use in the sculptures. As one of the goals of the project, connecting the art to the community was of utmost importance, noted resident artist Sabine LeDieu. However, so was the importance of increasing the community's awareness of environmental issues and recycling.

Ultimately, the cost of each sculpture was approximately $7,000, which included studio time, transportation costs, and additional materials needed to affix the bottle caps to the frame of the sculpture. Thankfully, the costs were defrayed based on the support of the grant-funded program. However, the lessons learned by the students were priceless.

COMMON CORE STATE STANDARDS

5,6,7,8.SL.1	Engage effectively in a range of collaborative discussions with diverse partners on grade level topics, texts, and issues, building on others' ideas and expressing their own clearly.
5,6,7,8.SL.2	Interpret information presented in diverse media and formats and explain how it contributes to a topic, text, or issue under study.
5,6,7,8.SL.5	Include multimedia components and visual displays in presentations to clarify information.

Technology Integration

Students communicated via Facebook and texting to share ongoing information regarding the project. Interactive QR codes accompany each sculpture and link to text information about the art installation and tips on recycling.

Teacher Reflection

"Joining students in studio to work together towards the goal of making environmentally themed public sculpture was rewarding for the youth, myself, and the community at large. While working together, we were able to share our thoughts about various environmental issues that face us in our community today. Students were empowered to make a statement about their investment in environmental stewardship, using public sculpture as their voice. While we worked side by side toward the common goal of manipulating materials we would use in our sculptures, we were able to casually throw out ideas and challenge ideas regarding 'reduce-reuse-recycle' (R3) and how we embrace or ignore this fundamental environmental call to action in our homes, schools, and community.

"I heard stories from the students and their teachers about how the youth involved in this project would start conversations about the environment, and specifically R3, with their families, their educators, and their peers. When we unveiled the sculptures, some of the participants made public speeches and were able to articulate how they worked to make their sculpture, why it was important to them, and share their views on R3 with adults, the press, and their community. The sculptures that we have created and installed in our community greet us each day, helping to start conversations and remind us of our responsibility to make good choices for our environment and our communities."—Sabine LeDieu

Jammin' with the Generals

Doug Wilson and Heather Smith
Jackson County High School
McKee, Kentucky

School Background

The school district is situated in the foothills of the Appalachian Mountains and is located 75 miles south of Lexington. This rural district services just over 2,100 students and has a mission to "accommodate the individualized learning needs of all students."

Challenging Investigation

How can we encourage an increased usage of the community's commercial kitchen?

Authentic Learning Experience Description

Doug Wilson, an agricultural science teacher, was interested in a farm-to-school initiative and in designing ways his students could bring their own created foods to the public. In a joint field trip to the local commercial kitchen that was built several years ago from funding via a tobacco court settlement, the agricultural students and the family consumer science students of Heather Smith toured the facility in the hopes that the students would desire to use the kitchen in the future. This trip spurred the students' idea for their answer to the challenging investigation. Students decided to promote the use of the community kitchen through the creation of their own goods for sale at the local farmers' market. While the eventual goal was to grow all the ingredients for and produce a salsa, students chose instead to start this Authentic Learning Experience with the leftover strawberries and apples that had already been purchased for a school fund-raiser. In creating the 1,100 jars of strawberry jam and 200 jars of applesauce, students had to use science and math to create the correct content percentages of sugar to fruit. Through the development of their recipe production, as part of the justification process, students also took Brix measurement readings, pH readings, and temperature readings as they learned about the science behind their cooking. Furthermore, students went beyond the mere cooking process and created a marketing plan for the sale of the strawberry jam, as well as coming up with a product name and designing a label. The products were labeled "Jammin' with the Generals" as a tribute to their school mascot. Students had to investigate the necessary FDA elements for the label to ensure they were compliant with required code before the jam could be marketed and sold. Additionally, students had to determine production costs, forecast profit margins, and develop their own sales strategy for their products. Throughout this process, students produced a written reflection in order to prepare for anticipated media events and interviews that would follow.

Students ultimately were afforded the opportunity of an outside audience that went beyond the mere customers at the farmers' market. A reporter from *USA Today* interviewed the students, as did the local television station. Additionally, students participated in a display at the Kentucky State Fair, and the experience was included in the state farmers' market brochure that is produced by the Kentucky Department of Agriculture. In a true community connection, additional schools in the community have utilized the commercial kitchen for projects modeled after the Jammin' with the Generals activity, as have other community organizations and extension services. FCS teacher Heather Smith also noted the career connection for her students, saying, "Having commercial facilities accessible to our students improves our ability to teach the culinary and marketing skills that our students need in order to be successful on our senior-level state exams."

COMMON CORE STATE STANDARDS

12.W.4	Produce clear and coherent writing in which the development, organization, and style are appropriate to task, purpose, and audience.
12.SL.1	Initiate and participate effectively in a range of collaborative discussions (one-on-one, in groups, teacher-led) with diverse partners on grades 11–12 topics, texts, and issues, building on others' ideas and expressing their own clearly and persuasively.
12.SL.4	Present information, findings, and supporting evidence, conveying a clear and distinct perspective, such that listeners can follow the line of reasoning, alternative or opposing perspectives are addressed, and the organization, development, substance, and style are appropriate to purpose, audience, and a range of formal and informal tasks.
S.IC.4	Use data from a sample survey to estimate a population mean or proportion; develop a margin of error through the use of simulation models for random sampling.

S.IC.6	Evaluate reports based on data.
S.MD.5	Weigh the possible outcomes of a decision by assigning probabilities to payoff values and finding expected values.
S.MD.7	Analyze decisions and strategies using probability concepts (e.g., product testing).

Technology Integration

Technology was not a part of this experience, however, it could easily be adapted to include QR codes on the jars of strawberry jam, or a graphic design class could be employed to create the labels for the jam.

Teacher Reflection

"This was a tremendous opportunity for our students to utilize a beautiful and functional facility here in our county. I have been very proud of our kids, our program, and this experience. I, and Heather, could not begin to imagine all the publicity this project would generate and how much the kids would take from the overall experience. This was truly one of the most rewarding teaching experiences I have been associated with."—Doug Wilson

CHAPTER 4

— ■ —

Justification of One's Work

In everyday life, we must make choices. Decisions might be made on the spur of the moment or they may require more thought. However, in either case, you have to justify your actions. Perhaps justification is needed only for yourself, or maybe it is necessary for others that are closely affected by your choices. At the highest level, the work that we complete requires us to provide a rationale for our thought process. This is certainly true for most job-related decisions and is especially true for jobs that require innovation and creativity. For those of you reading this, you are probably already thinking about your lesson plans or curriculums that you have developed. Whether you had to justify your work to your administrative team or a new curriculum had to be approved by the school board, you probably already have a foundational understanding in regard to the Authentic Learning Experience element of justification.

Moving Beyond Brainstorming

We frequently ask our students to brainstorm ideas. Often this process is simply a byproduct of a designated activity. By this, I mean that the brainstorming process has very little guidance. Students might brainstorm a possible solution to making the line in the cafeteria move more quickly or ways in which airlines could more efficiently seat passengers, but they rarely go beyond the list of possible ideas. Perhaps a discussion on why the possible ideas may work might follow, but there is a need to provide a further development of the brainstorming session. Students must practice, develop, and refine ways in which they can justify their conclusions. We must provide them with the tools to do this and require them to do it.

Teachers typically operate on the assumption that a group may produce more ideas than an individual, and I was certainly no exception for a large portion of my career. However, I now like to start with individual brainstorming. We all have those students who like to dominate the conversation, and we certainly all have those students who don't participate at all. In order to negate this possibility, I build individual brainstorming into the process before small-group and larger-group sharing occur. This creates the context for individual processing of ideas, helps in the pre-assessment of current knowledge, and ensures all ideas may be heard before one or two students attempt to take over the process. Of course, ground rules (see Figure 4.1, below) still must be established before embarking on the group portion of the brainstorming session to maximize the individual ideas that are then contributed to the group as a whole.

Figure 4.1: Ground Rules for Brainstorming Sessions

- Bring a minimum of three individual ideas to the table before group sharing.
- Move beyond the obvious.
- Treat everyone as an equal contributor.
- Take turns.
- Don't judge.
- No idea is a bad idea.
- All ideas are recorded.
- There is no one right answer.
- All possibilities can lead to amazing results.
- Remember that every great solution started as a tiny idea.

Ensuring students are prepared to comprehend the need to justify all of their proposed solutions to the challenging investigation requires scaffolding on our part. Entrenching students in valuable brainstorming sessions is a start to that scaffolding process. Consider using the activities listed in Figure 4.2 (page 59) for developing the brainstorming process. Adapt the activities as needed to fit your grade level and content area.

Figure 4.2   Content Area Brainstorming Activities

SUBJECT	BRAINSTORMING ACTIVITY
Social Studies/ History	As a class, choose five major inventions of the past 200 years. First, have individuals do the following: 1. Explain why each is a major invention and how it has changed life as we know it. 2. Determine three ways life would be different if each invention were never created. Explain how that change would directly impact you for better and for worse. Now, have small groups of three students work together to compare their answers. Note: The activity could be tailored to different kinds of social studies classes. (In a government class, have students focus on constitutional amendments; in a sociology class, have students focus on stereotypes, and so on.)
Math	Have individual students journal about their relationship with math on a daily basis. (This can be specific to your math course—geometry, algebra, etc.) Remind students that complete sentences are necessary and explanations must accompany the descriptions. Partner students to compare their findings. Then combine two pairs of students to make further comparisons.
ELA	Read a short story to the class. Conduct a class discussion on the role of the main character. Have groups of three students do the following: 1. Individually rewrite a specific section of the story from the perspective of a minor character that now becomes the main character, with each student taking a different section of the story but using the same character. 2. Have students work as a group to make sense of their individually written sections to create an overall new story. 3. Have a class discussion on the process of writing the new stories and a comparison of the groups' creations.
Science	Assign small groups of students one of the following topics: water, energy, food security, poverty, health, and climate change. Have individual students brainstorm ways in which the appropriate content area (chemistry, biology, etc.) can be applied to the assigned topic to help solve a given problem surrounding our global future. Individual ideas are shared with the group, and arguments are made for the best ideas to produce for the class at large.
Art or Music	Split students into groups of four or five. Have one person in the group start a drawing. The individual drawing continues for three to five minutes. At the end of the timed period, the drawing is passed to the next person in the group for another round of three to five minutes of drawing. This process is repeated until all members of the group have contributed to the drawing. At the conclusion of the drawing session, students work together to create a story about the drawing based on the collaborative work that was completed. The application in a music class would similarly have students either write or perform music, depending on the advanced level of the course.

SUBJECT	BRAINSTORMING ACTIVITY
Foreign Language	Similar to the above description of the art or music class, students in any level foreign language class could apply the same principles to developing a written conversation, or a short story for higher-level classes, in which students build on one another's writing to complete the task. Again, a debriefing session of all involved should follow the activity.
Health	Assign students to groups of five, with each student taking on an individual role (pharmaceutical representative, physician, senior citizen, family member on welfare, legislative representative). Have members brainstorm how the rising healthcare costs affect them personally based on their assigned roles. Then each individual must devise three possible solutions to decrease the costs of healthcare, providing an explanation for each solution. All group members come together to compare their ideas and analyze the effects of the solutions on society.
Physical Education	This is similar to the process for art and music students. One student in a group could create a segment to a physical fitness routine. The next student in the group would have to build on the previous group member's activity. The final version of the completed routine, once all group members have added a section, would be reviewed for continuity and effectiveness.

Many of the activities listed in Figure 4.2 could be developed into the greater context of an Authentic Learning Experience. The provided activities would be appropriate for use in the scaffolding process as students gain a greater understanding of the brainstorming process and an improved grasp of the content. For instance, the example provided for the health course is merely a simulation, but it could be further implemented to incorporate a focus on true change. The students could use the brainstorming process to determine an overall focus for either the class or for each smaller group of students. This focus or the focus points could be used to create a formal presentation for any number of experts. A written proposal could be submitted to one expert, or a panel of experts could be invited in for a presentation. The experts might include a local legislator, a member of a healthcare-focused group such as Healthcare Professionals for Healthcare Reform, and perhaps a professional in the medical insurance field. Throughout the process of conducting the experience, students might create and administer a survey to the public about people's experiences with healthcare over the last decade and analyze the public's views on the impact that the most recent healthcare reform laws have had on them as individuals. Thus, not only would the Common Core standards for writing, speaking, and listening be included in this experience but also the math standards related to probability and statistics would be as well. This activity might also meet a variety of state standards. For example, in my state of Pennsylvania, this experience would include the standards for assessing factors that impact adult health consumer choices and analyzing the interrelationships between environmental factors and community health. Throughout the immersion of this experience, students would certainly have to include the justification of their findings and would do so through much of their analysis and research.

☑ **Check for Understanding**

Choose any of the activities described in Figure 4.2 and brainstorm a list of possible Authentic Learning Experiences that could be developed from the given activity. Have a teaching partner do the same. Compare your possible designs and then work together to fully develop the experience based on the design principles explained in Chapters 1–6.

Making the Most Out of Research

Research papers used to be a major annoyance for me as a student, and I'm sure plenty of students would agree with my sentiments! I was a history major in college, but even before then, growing up just outside of Blacksburg, Virginia, in the early 1990s, I'd spend hours in the Virginia Tech library conducting research for my high school classes. Microfilm was a horror, and the Internet was something that was apparently still a dream of Al Gore's. In all honesty, I don't think I could tell you anything about what I researched, what my thesis statements might have been, or even what I concluded about my research. I only vaguely recall something about the POWs of the Vietnam War. However, as much as I realized how little of a lasting effect the researching process had on me, as a teacher I certainly provided numerous opportunities for my students to conduct research in the same vein. It wasn't until a few years into my career that I made the shift to making research have meaning.

Yes, researching skills are needed, should be developed, and must be included in our curriculum no matter what grade level or content area we teach. However, the way in which research is applied in the classroom is of debatable importance. Merely having students answer our challenging investigation without requiring any justification for the determined outcome doesn't mean much in the context of authenticity. In fact, without justification, students aren't doing much more than brainstorming or simply repeating a possible answer they found through a quick online search. Thus, it is necessary to not only require students to justify their outcomes but also to scaffold the research process itself. The steps in the justification process are shown in Figure 4.3 (below).

Figure 4.3   The Justification Process

- Gather data.
- Develop a hypothesis.
- Weigh possibilities.
- Validate sources and suppositions.
- Determine a target solution.
- Consult expert opinions.
- Reevaluate.
- Finalize conclusions.

True research is about applying one's ability to think critically. In this case, it will certainly help you to review the critical-thinking discussion and activities discussed in Chapter 2. However, it is important to think about research as more than simply finding information. Think about research as taking that newly found information, manipulating that information, and using that information to support a possible answer to the challenging investigation.

The research process should first be about procuring data. In some instances, data is collected through interaction with the community via surveys, logs, and observations over time. In other instances, data may come from expert sources that have already gathered the facts and figures. It is up to our students to utilize the data, analyze the data, compare the data, and ultimately present the data as a source of justification for their end products or solutions. Charts and graphs are the norm in this portion of the researching process. Thus, it is important to incorporate math into your course no matter what content area you actually teach. Keep in mind that if math is not your strong suit, you can always look to your math colleagues for guidance in this area.

It is advisable for the management of time to begin students with a series of websites to explore as they embark on their research. This, too, will ensure students aren't merely haphazardly searching on the Internet for sources of information. Databases are a great place to have students start this research and the analysis of the information (see Figure 4.4, below). Doing so will also help students weigh possibilities as they validate sources and conclusions presented in the research. Additionally, as students move beyond the merely brainstormed possible solutions to the challenging investigation, they will begin to fully develop their own hypotheses and determine target solutions. However, the process doesn't end there. Students will continue to develop their research, consult experts, and reevaluate their work in order to be fully prepared for the justification of their ultimate answer to the challenging investigation.

Figure 4.4   Useful Online Databases

- United Nations . . . . www.un.org/en/databases
- ProCon.org . . . . www.procon.org
- FactCheck.org. . . . . www.factcheck.org
- OpenSecrets.org . . . . .www.opensecrets.org
- Opposing Viewpoints in Context*www.gale.cengage.com/InContext/viewpoints.htm

* Offered by Gale Cengage Learning with a paid subscription

You can't stress to your students enough the need to back up all of their determinations with the research collected. However, it is also important to teach students how to evaluate information. Again, this is where the scaffolding process factors into the facilitation of the Authentic Learning Experience. You may have to explicitly teach these methods of evaluation to some or all of your students. At the very least, you will need to assess their ability to evaluate information before you begin. Use the suggested activities in Figure 4.5 (page 64) to help plan the lessons to scaffold the justification process.

Figure 4.5   Scaffolding Activities to Teach the Justification Process

JUSTIFICATION PROCESS	SCAFFOLDING ACTIVITIES
Gather data	Have small groups of students develop a survey about any general topic related to your content area of study. (For example, in a health class unit on nutrition, student groups could create surveys related to fast-food, fresh vegetable, or soda consumption.) Have each group distribute its survey to the class and construct a graph that visually represents the collected data.
Develop a hypothesis	Discuss the difference between observations and hypotheses. Give students specific examples of each. Choose a journal article related to your content and appropriate for your grade level that exhibits both observation and hypothesis examples. Have students read the article independently and highlight the observation examples in one color and the hypothesis examples in another color. Have student partners compare their findings. Review the article as a class.
Weigh possibilities	Have students work with partners. Give each pair of students a "Choose Your Own Adventure" type of activity that is related to the content of study. Have students work together to determine which path they will take. Students must make a list of pros and cons for making each choice. The determined path must be accounted for based on the pro/con list created.
Validate sources and suppositions	Present small groups of students with three websites containing similar content to review. Have each student review one site and present his or her findings to the rest of the group. Have the groups compare information and determine differing points of view. As a group, have the students find two or three additional sites to support any information gathered. (Try using Wikipedia, a database, and an academic journal site for a variety of sources and reliability.)
Determine a target solution	Give students a problem related to your content area. Provide students with several possible solutions to the problem. Have each student choose a solution individually and provide a written explanation for his or her choice. Group students according to their choices. Have groups work together to create a convincing argument for their choice. Next, have student groups present their arguments. Finally, after all presentations have concluded, have students choose one other solution to debunk and one other solution to support. Written explanations must accompany this process.
Consult expert opinions	Have each student work with a partner to review an interview of an expert in your content area. This could be a recorded video interview or a written copy of an interview. Conduct a class discussion surrounding the questions asked of the expert to develop a list of requirements when consulting experts.

JUSTIFICATION PROCESS	SCAFFOLDING ACTIVITIES
Reevaluate	Choose a controversial current event related to your content area. Have students list all the information they know about the event. Provide students with an article about the event, and have students individually determine the details surrounding the current status of the event. Provide students with a minimum of three articles written about the same current event. Have small groups of students work together to compare the stories and reevaluate their original beliefs after reading each of the articles. Note: Articles from different sources such as www.cnn.com, www.washingtonpost.com, and www.foxnews.com will provide different perspectives.
Finalize conclusions	Give small teams of students an outcome related to your unit of study, and provide the students with five or six charts, graphs, and tables. Have students determine which items help support the given outcome and provide an explanation related to the support.

Now that you have created your open-ended challenging investigation that has either a community or a career connection, it becomes necessary to require that students justify all the work that they complete and the final answers they propose for the challenge. Learn from the meaningful ways in which the following examples required students to be deeply involved in the justification element as a part of their Authentic Learning Experience.

Sample Authentic Learning Experiences

Portrait of an Artist

Rebecca Mason
Conservatory Lab Charter School
Boston, Massachusetts

School Background

Conservatory Lab Charter School is an Expeditionary Learning School that focuses on student achievement through "academic, creative, and social success in a music-infused curriculum." Not only is music integrated throughout the academic curriculum, but students are also exposed to weekly listening experiences focusing on different music genres and receive direct music instruction in choral and orchestral programs.

Challenging Investigation

How can I create a self-portrait that shows what is special about me?

Authentic Learning Experience Description

Students spent three months conducting this two-part Authentic Learning Experience. The first phase of the experience focused on color, medium, tools, and techniques. Students viewed various works of art, listened to music related to different colors, and created their own art using a variety of mediums. During the month-long study of color, the classroom was transformed into a revolving art exhibit in which each day a new artist was put on display. Students experimented with mixing colors and created their own color wheels. Color books were created to link words with colors. Students also produced their own replication of Pablo Picasso's *Three Musicians* to show their mastery of color techniques and use of artist's tools. This masterpiece was displayed at the entrance of the school, creating part of the community connection. The rest of the school and visitors to the school became part of the outside audience.

Students moved into the second phase of the experience as they listened to stories, both fiction and nonfiction, about various artists. These artists included Andy Warhol, Frida Kahlo, and Pierre-Auguste Renoir, among others. This process helped the students to understand how to use color and detail to tell a story through a self-portrait. Students then completed a full-body self-portrait to incorporate math into the experience. Students measured themselves, with the help of the first-grade class, against nonstandard objects such as toy cars. This connected the concepts of ratios and proportions for student understanding.

The final self-portraits were done on canvas. Students used sketchbooks to help further develop their understanding of proportions and spatial differences within facial features, as they used a mirror to draw their reflections. Students partnered with an expert fine artist to again experiment with colors and pigments of their skin. Students had to revise their work over the course of the immersion in this process. Ultimately, through the continued use of the sketchbooks and work with the artist, the students went through a process of reflection and justification before finalizing their self-portraits on canvas.

The portraits were ultimately put on display in the school's entry vestibule as a welcome to all school visitors. To prepare for their display, students made a trip to the Boston Institute of Contemporary Art. Students noted the exhibits and artists' statements. The students returned from the trip and dictated their own artist statements to accompany their portraits in order to fully answer the challenging investigation. Parents and community members were invited to the exhibit opening as another outside audience for the work that the students so carefully completed. Students also created self-portrait books and self-portrait postcards as extensions of this Authentic Learning Experience.

COMMON CORE STATE STANDARDS

K.RIT.1	With prompting and support, ask and answer questions about key details in a text.
K.RIT.7	With prompting and support, describe the relationship between illustrations and the text in which they appear (e.g., what person, place, thing, or idea in the text an illustration depicts).
K.RIT.9	With prompting and support, identify basic similarities in and differences between two texts on the same topic (e.g., in illustrations, descriptions, or procedures).
K.RIT.10	Actively engage in group reading activities with purpose and understanding.
K.SL.1	Participate in collaborative conversations with diverse partners about kindergarten topics and texts with peers and adults in small and larger groups.

K.SL.2	Confirm understanding of a text read aloud or information presented orally or through other media by asking and answering questions about key details and requesting clarification if something is not understood.
K.SL.5	Add drawings or other visual displays to descriptions as desired to provide additional detail.
K.SL.6	Speak audibly and express thoughts, feelings, and ideas clearly.
K.MD.1	Describe measureable attributes of objects, such as length or weight. Describe several measurable attributes of a single object.
K.MD.2	Directly compare two objects with a measurable attribute in common, to see which object has "more of"/"less of" the attribute, and describe the difference. For example, directly compare the heights of two children and describe one child as taller/shorter.
K.G.1	Describe objects in the environment using names of shapes, and describe the relative positions of these objects using terms such as *above, below, beside, in front of, behind,* and *next to.*
K.G.5	Model shapes in the world by building shapes from components (e.g., sticks and clay balls) and drawing shapes.

Technology Integration

Technology was not an integral part of this experience. However, in a classroom that has access to iPads or other tablets, one might consider incorporating drawing apps that have the playback feature. In this instance, students could practice drawing and visually review the drawing in stages, providing an explanation for each stage.

Teacher Reflection

"The Portrait of an Artist study is one of the most exciting and ambitious themes I have endeavored to experience with young learners. The topic came out of my own love of fine art, which paired well with a preschooler's desire to tell their own story and demonstrate their growing skill in as many different creative forms as possible. Over the years of working with this theme, I have become more enterprising with the individual projects, though the overall intentions remain the same: help the children to create high-quality representations of themselves while communicating their unique perspective to the world. I have found that my own ability to communicate expectations and model techniques has also improved the level of skill and quality in the children's work. My own learning process, as the presenter of this grand topic, has also been informed by the many resources that I have discovered about this topic, from video clips on the Internet, to amazing children's books about artists, to music that evokes emotional journeys and connects to color and rhythm. As long as I am a teacher of young children, I will endeavor to experience this incredible study with the next generation of artists, musicians, and scholars."—Becca Mason

Empowering Children

Benjamin Stern
The Emery/Weiner School
Houston, Texas

School Background

This private Jewish day school in the city of Houston mainly services upper middle-class students. Students are afforded the opportunity to use a lot of technology in their coursework, as many classrooms have a laptop cart of computers and the district is moving toward a full Bring Your Own Device model.

Challenging Investigation

How can we help to effect enduring, positive change with a political, social, or economic problem in Africa?

Authentic Learning Experience Description

The catalyst for this experience was a mere hope to begin a pen pal exchange program with a school in Africa, all the while studying the origins of the African colonial period and the issues related to the European takeover of much of the continent. While surfing the website ePals in search of a connection with a school in Africa, teacher Ben Stern was fortunate to link to Ibrahim Kamara and the Empowering Children and Youth School (ECYS) in Freetown, Sierra Leone. Kamara, Stern discovered, was a 22-year-old former child soldier who was working to give back to the disadvantaged youth who were much like he had been years before. Kamara had already raised money to empower the ECYS with new teachers and a new building. However, when the students at Emery/Weiner learned about Kamara's amazing journey, they wanted to do more than simply be pen pals with the ECYS students. They wanted to give much more to the community in Freetown and now had a clear path to solving their challenging investigation.

Students continued to research the current issues in Sierra Leone related to the colonial influence from decades past. Students consulted experts in the field and contacted various nongovernmental organizations (NGOs) to discover firsthand what was facing their peers at ECYS. Students applied the lessons learned from the colonial period and the effects of colonization to justify their choices on how to help the community in Freetown. Additionally, realizing the impact that technology had made on their own education, students determined they wanted to help to bring technology into the lives of the students at ECYS. In order to do this, students first had to face an outside audience, the board of trustees for their own school, to get approval for their fund-raising efforts. After students presented to the board of trustees, they were not only afforded the opportunity to begin their own fund-raising efforts, but the board was so impressed with their dedication, learning, and motivation that many members presented students with personal checks and also donated individual laptops.

During the course of the fund-raising efforts, students organized themselves into a variety of groups to ensure their efforts would be a success. These groups included students in charge of finances, social media, and the communication with the ECYS students, as well as project leaders. Students also took it upon themselves to contact experts for help in a variety of aspects of the experiences, which included contacting those who knew about social media to help publicize their efforts, including starting a Facebook page and a Twitter account to promote their efforts.

The ECYS students sent one hundred pieces of handmade jewelry from their own community to be sold as part of the fund-raiser. Students ultimately were able to raise $6,500, which was enough money to install many technology changes for ECYS. However, Emery/Weiner students had to determine the best way that they could help ECYS and did so through a series of regular meetings between the three classes involved in this endeavor. Ultimately, the decision was made to pay for one year's worth of rent on the school, purchase five new MacBook computers, and pay for an Internet connection for the school. In addition to the fund-raising efforts and purchase of needed items for ECYS, students in both schools created a video documentary of their schools and communities to exchange with each other.

COMMON CORE STATE STANDARDS

8.RIT.3	Analyze how a text makes connections among and distinctions between individuals, ideas, or events.
8.RIT.6	Determine an author's point of view or purpose in a text and analyze how the author acknowledges and responds to conflicting evidence or viewpoints.
8.RIT.9	Analyze a case in which two or more texts provide conflicting information on the same topic and identify where the texts disagree on matters of fact or interpretation.

8.W.1	Write arguments to support claims with clear reasons and relevant evidence.
8.W.7	Conduct short research projects to answer a question (including a self-generated question), drawing on several sources and generating additional related, focused questions that allow for multiple avenues of exploration.
8.W.9	Draw evidence from literary or informational texts to support analysis, reflection, and research.
8.SL.4	Present claims and findings, emphasizing salient points in a focused, coherent manner with relevant evidence, sound valid reasoning, and well-chosen details; use appropriate eye contact, adequate volume, and clear pronunciation.
8.SL.5	Integrate multimedia and visual displays into presentations to clarify information, strengthen claims and evidence, and add interest.

Technology Integration

Students relied heavily on Skype to interact with their African peers. Additionally, as several classes were working on the same goal for this experience, students utilized Google Drive for collaboration. Students also used a Facebook app to promote the sale of the African jewelry for the fund-raising efforts.

Teacher Reflection

"The students themselves deserve enormous credit. They came up with the good ideas; we [the teachers] just helped them figure out how to implement them. The students' ability to work together, to dream big, to identify what they needed to learn, to consult experts, and to care about real-world issues in the first place was a consequence of the skills cultivated throughout the year. Advocates of this style of instruction often forget how important it is to slowly build the skills necessary to implement it. Students who are accustomed to a very linear and straightforward class need the time to transition to this more independent framework. Yet once students have these skills, they are able to take advantage of this freedom. When they can own their learning in this way, students achieve considerably more than they can in a traditional classroom, as we see in this example.

"More than anything else, it is a certain sort of school culture that yields results like these. Community service and moral character are among Emery/Weiner's chief institutional values. Teachers have high expectations for their students. When excellence is defined by real-world impacts rather than letter grades, kids do amazing things."—Benjamin Stern

Honduras 2012, Children Changing the World

Brian Copes
Calera High School
Calera, Alabama

School Background

Calera is a small, rural school district that houses grades 7–12 in the high school. Technology isn't always readily available, but due to the sole efforts of teacher Brian Copes, Calera High School has recently been named one of the top fifteen PRIME (Partnership Response in Manufacturing Education) schools in the U.S. by the Society of Manufacturing Engineers.

Challenging Investigation

How can we make a real difference in the lives of those less fortunate than us in an effort to truly change the world?

Authentic Learning Experience Description

After reading the staggering statistics regarding the billions of people who live on less than $2.50 a day and the poor conditions that many in the world face, students in Brian Copes's pre-engineering class knew they had to do something to make a dent in the statistics. According to Copes, he could have had his students work on anything related to the mechanics of engineering, such as "pimping out a golf cart," but that would have been less than meaningful and certainly wouldn't have contributed to making the lives of those living in third-world countries any better. Instead, students embarked on the challenging investigation where they worked to design low-cost basic utility vehicles (BUVs) to be used in areas of the world with poor road access. During this stage, students worked to develop a kind of BUV that could be replicated in the jungles of remote villages. Through the justification process, students could only use tools that would be found in these areas around the world. Thus, simple hand tools were chosen in order to be able to replicate the process once on location. This design even won first place in the Institute for Affordable Transportation's design competition, beating out the team from Purdue University.

Simultaneously, after a challenge was posed to students from a class guest speaker, they worked on designing and fashioning prosthetic legs from old car parts. The desire was to meet the needs of those in third-world countries who can't afford prosthetic legs and certainly don't have health insurance to cover the necessary costs. Students worked with Next Step Prosthetics & Orthotics in Alabaster, Alabama, to make expert connections and work through the justification of their design process to ensure the limbs were ergonomically correct and could be properly fitted to those in need. Students used 1989 Toyota Corolla motor mounts for both the ankle and knee joints. They hope to extend the use of these inexpensive and repurposed limbs to many of the people who became amputees as a result of the massive 2010 earthquake in Haiti.

The class then made a connection with the nonprofit Projecto Honduras to take their knowledge and their creations to a true outside audience, a remote village in Honduras during a 2012 summer trip. Once there, students were split into two teams to carry out their work in giving back to the global community. One team worked with Adam Williams, the owner of Next Step, to fit amputees in the Honduran jungle with the prosthetic legs they designed and created. The students successfully fitted fourteen amputees with the prosthetics they made for an approximate cost of $200 (versus the $3,000 to $60,000 typical prosthetics cost in the United States). The other team worked with the BUVs. These disassembled BUVs had been shipped in containers donated by Dole. Once on location, the Calera students instructed local Honduran teens how to assemble the BUVs. These vehicles were then put to use as ambulances in a remote area that was accessible only by a rope bridge that spanned a river and was a two-day journey on foot from the nearest medical help. This amazing effort in giving, teaching, and learning was documented by the film company Magnolialand Entertainment with the intent to distribute the documentary to every high school in Alabama. The documentary was designed to be an inspirational tool to motivate classrooms around the state to create meaning through learning. At the time of this publication, the funding for distribution is still in process. The Society of Manufacturing Engineers will be helping with a nationwide distribution of the documentary.

The work of these students has reached far beyond what they ever could have imagined. Copes and his students also worked with DeepRock Manufacturing in creating a well-drilling attachment for the student-designed vehicles, as the area of Honduras that they visited had more than 120 communities without fresh running water. The Honduran mayor of the region hired local Hondurans to operate the vehicles and drill for fresh water in these areas. Additionally, three of Copes's students are now planning on studying biomedical engineering at the collegiate level in a true career connection with the Authentic Learning Experience.

COMMON CORE STATE STANDARDS

12.W.2	Write informative/explanatory texts to examine and convey complex ideas, concepts, and information clearly and accurately through the effective selection, organization, and analysis of content.
12.W.4	Produce clear and coherent writing in which the development, organization, and style are appropriate to task, purpose, and audience.
12.W.5	Develop and strengthen writing as needed by planning, revising, editing, rewriting, or trying a new approach, focusing on addressing what is most significant for a specific purpose and audience.
12.W.7	Conduct short as well as more sustained research projects to answer a question (including a self-generated question) or solve a problem; narrow or broaden the inquiry when appropriate; synthesize multiple sources on the subject, demonstrating understanding of the subject under investigation.
12.SL.1	Initiate and participate effectively in a range of collaborative discussions with diverse partners on grades 11–12 topics, texts, and issues, building on others' ideas and expressing their own clearly and persuasively.
12.SL.4	Present information, findings, and supporting evidence, conveying a clear and distinct perspective, such that listeners can follow the line of reasoning, alternative or opposing perspectives are addressed, and the organization, development, substance, and style are appropriate to purpose, audience, and a range of formal and informal tasks.
G.CO.12	Make formal geometric constructions with a variety of tools and methods (compass and straightedge, string, reflective devices, paper folding, dynamic geometric software, etc.).
G.MG.1	Use geometric shapes, their measures, and their properties to describe objects (e.g., modeling a tree trunk or human torso as a cylinder).
G.MG.2	Apply concepts of density based on area and volume in modeling situations (e.g., persons per square mile, BTUs per cubic foot).
G.MG.3	Apply geometric methods to solve design problems (e.g., designing an object or structure to satisfy physical constraints or minimize cost).
G.GMD.4	Identify the shapes of two-dimensional cross-sections of three-dimensional objects, and identify three-dimensional objects generated by rotations of two-dimensional objects.
S.MD.7	Analyze decisions and strategies using probability concepts (e.g., product testing, medical testing, pulling a hockey goalie at the end of a game).

Technology Integration

Copes believes in "working with what we have." After the construction of a new high school provided him with a basketball court–sized shop but no equipment with which to fill it, the students certainly had to make do! Other than the use of SolidWorks, a 3-D computer-aided design program, technology use was extremely limited in the execution of this experience.

Teacher Reflection

"My proudest moments are when my students take what they have learned in the classroom to help others and change the world of complete strangers. My amazing students have invented utility vehicles designed to drill for life-giving fresh water, plow fields to grow crops, and serve as ambulances to save countless lives in underdeveloped countries. My students invented a prosthetic leg out of simple used automotive parts. Impressed and invigorated, the Calera community rallied with me in a fund-raising effort to take ten students to Honduras, where they fitted fourteen amputees with the prosthetic legs that they had invented in class.

"While in Honduras, after the first amputee to be fit with a prosthetic leg took his maiden steps, a beaming student exclaimed, 'Mr. Copes, it's a miracle!' I choked back my tears. Later, a woman came up crying and thanking the students. She explained that when her husband had lost his leg, he lost his livelihood, his self-worth, and his desire to live because he could no longer provide for his family. The tearful woman further explained that when her husband was fitted with my students' leg, it was the first time since his accident that he had smiled. Her husband regained his dignity and desire to live. These experiences cannot be taught in the traditional classroom, and these 'WOW!' moments profoundly changed the lives of everyone blessed to be involved."—Brian Copes

CHAPTER 5

—— ■ ——

Creating a Meaningful Outside Audience

No matter how well you have designed your Authentic Learning Experience based on the preceding three requirements, I can guarantee you will still have students who aren't engaged. However, while I could never purport that the full use of the design principles of Authentic Learning Experiences will engage every single student, including an outside audience will most certainly engage many more students! In fact, from my experience, I have been able to target nearly every student involved in my Authentic Learning Experiences. This includes my students who are gifted, have IEPs, are ELLs, and everyone in between. Simply having the knowledge that the final product will be placed on community public display, completed for expert review, or performed for a group of expert individuals has a powerful impact!

I often come across great learning experiences that stop short at the inclusion of an authentic audience. Instead of adding meaning and taking the experience to the next level, teachers have their students present only to their classmates. In fact, many Project-Based Learning publications state this is an acceptable "public audience," as students are showcasing their learning. Sure, students get practice in their presentation skills and improve their communication skills, but where is the meaning in the presentation? How does this truly showcase the hard work and often amazing results of the students' challenging investigation?

What Is a Meaningful Outside Audience?

Have you experienced demonstrations of learning where your students present by simply reading their PowerPoint slides? Perhaps you were more concerned with managing your students in the "audience" and their behavior than actually assessing the students presenting! Unfortunately, we have all experienced the typical book review, the iMovie extravaganza, or the proposal to persuade students to pick the best science fair project. I remember the agony of having to present my book reviews in the eleventh grade and the boredom on the faces of my peers as I discussed *Jane Eyre*. I also remember, in the early stages of my own career, having students showcase their knowledge of a variety of African countries as they tried to convince prospective "tourists," their peers, to travel to their assigned countries. Unfortunately, I don't remember much about the intricacies of the plot of *Jane Eyre*, and I can almost say with certainty that my former students remember very little about those African countries. However, my law students who participated in our Crime Board Authentic Learning Experience, in which they presented their proposals on how to reduce crime in our county to a panel of experts, most certainly remember the learning that took place during the course of their challenging investigation. The panel included the head of the county prison board, a representative from the district attorney's office, a state congressional representative, a police officer, a police chief, and a district justice. Once, when a class revealed to the panel that our county had only a small percentage of our eligible prison population participating in a rehabilitation program, a debate ensued between a local legislator and a representative from the district attorney's office. Another time, when the head of the prison board promised the students he would take their idea of creating a prison garden to the rest of the board, the students were truly engaged in the learning process. My students were professional, proud, and, best of all, heard!

How to Create an Outside Audience

Moving beyond presenting to one's classmates and teachers can require baby steps. Before I felt comfortable with using a panel of experts, I started with having my students present to other classes. I found that the level of engagement increased slightly and the final products improved somewhat. However, in order to make the experience undeniably authentic in nature, we must be prepared to take the leap outside of the realm of comfort and present our students with the opportunity to truly showcase their learning, critical thinking, and innovation.

An outside audience can take many different forms. I always like to invite a panel of experts to listen to formal presentations from my students at least once during their time in my class. Making these expert connections can be time-consuming, but it is well worth the effort. The best place to start is by asking your fellow staff members and even your students if they have any connections to the experts who are needed. I have had the good fortune of having a career counselor in my building who has made many of the connections for me. I have also resorted to Internet searches for local experts and have had positive results from cold calls. Community members, civic leaders, and business partners of the district in which you teach are often more than willing to make connections with your students and provide you with the audience you seek. Additional ideas on how to make expert connections can be found in Chapter 3.

☑ Check for Understanding

Create a list of possible expert contacts in your content area. Ask your teaching partners to do the same. Compare the lists. Determine which people may be the best fit for making actual contact.

In some instances, I have multiple small groups presenting to my outside audience. At other times, I have small groups present their possible ideas for the challenging investigation to the class that then move into a full class working together to create one overall presentation. If you teach multiple classes that require the same type of expert panel, or if you have several small groups within a class, you have several options to limit the potentially taxing nature of working with those experts. You can have several experts working together during a set time you have designated for the small groups' presentations. Each expert or pair of experts could be given a room where two or three small groups present during an hour or an hour-and-a-half time period. I use "in-house" field trip permission forms in order to allow students to miss a twenty- or thirty-minute portion of another class. You can also find multiple panels of experts to work each class. This is generally my choice for implementation when I have more than one class that is doing an overall presentation that involves every student. These presentations typically last forty-five minutes and follow with a question-and-answer session that may last the rest of the class period in a block schedule. (Non-block teachers can use the "in-house" field trip request mentioned earlier.) In either instance, overly extending your gratitude to the experts is imperative. A note of thanks or even a small luncheon is a wonderful token of appreciation for their efforts. Figure 5.1 (below) summarizes the keys to a successful exhibition.

Figure 5.1   Keys to a Successful Exhibition

- Leave the tri-fold poster boards at home.
- Send invitations to true content area experts and community members.
- Require student interaction with exhibition patrons.
- Schedule demonstrations of learning through experiments or presentations.

If bringing in a panel of experts is not something with which you are comfortable, create an exhibition of student work. This, too, takes time and planning, but is a way in which students are able to interact with experts, the community, and parents. The key, however, is to have real interaction between your students and those who attend the exhibition. Additionally, while parents deserve to view the learning of their students and we, as teachers, want to involve parents, for these exhibitions, in order to truly be authentic, you need to have experts and other community members involved. Certainly some subject areas lend themselves to this type of presentation of learning. Art exhibitions are a great example. However, remember that you must go back to the design principles of Authentic Learning Experiences in order to meet the other qualifications. Merely having a science fair where model solar systems are on display doesn't fit the criteria of Authentic Learning Experiences. A great example of art on exhibition comes from a former colleague of mine, Katlyn Wolfgang. In her sculpture class's partnership with Katie Sewell Anderson's tenth-grade English class, students created and displayed lifelike forms around the school in the style of the artist George Segal. The sculptures wore QR code "student IDs" that, when scanned, revealed a story written about the sculpture's life by the ELA students. Pieces of this interactive art exhibit were then taken into the community for viewing. Possible showcase locations are listed in Figure 5.2 (page 83).

If an exhibition sounds like something you might like to try but you aren't ready for the evening time commitment from yourself or your students, perhaps you might try a community exhibition. Find a local community business or civic organization that is willing to showcase the work

Figure 5.2   Possible Community Showcase Sites

- Historical society
- Library
- State capitol
- County courthouse
- Town square
- Art gallery
- Civic organizations
- Reception areas of business locations

of your students. While you may not be able to implement the interaction between the audience and your students, this is still a great way for students to showcase their work. Again, art is the best format for this type of exhibition, but perhaps your students produce documentaries that are showcased at the local historical society or writing that is promoted at the local library. You could include a request that those who view the work of your students leave feedback related to the final products. It is also advantageous, if possible, to provide students with the opportunity to staff these exhibits when feasible. This may be easier for older students who have their own transportation, but younger students could be involved in a field trip designated for this purpose. If it is going to be a requirement of the Authentic Learning Experience, however, ensure that all students have the opportunity to participate in this manner.

Presentations and exhibitions aren't the only way in which you can showcase the work of your students in an authentic way. Figure 5.3 (page 84) shows some of the ways you can have students present their work without face-to-face interaction. For example, having students send their final work to an expert via the mail is certainly acceptable. Perhaps the students write a final proposal and mail it to a government official or an expert in their field as a way to demonstrate their learning and to solicit feedback. The feedback may or may not come, and that's okay. It teaches your students that they can be proactive in life and interact with others in a meaningful way. While your students are almost certain to receive a response from a government official, that response from *Dateline NBC* may not occur! Maybe your students write a pitch to a company about a newly designed racing helmet they've created in physics class, or perhaps your environmental studies students write letters to their state representative voicing their concerns on the water quality of the local river and what approach should be taken to improve it. This process promotes civic responsibility and a call to action that many adults choose not to exercise. In any case, the anticipation of a possible response from mailing the letters or sending the online documents is a deep motivating factor for students. Remember the Authentic Learning Experience I described in the first chapter? The poorly written and grammatically incorrect letter my students received from a death row prisoner they truly believe is innocent was a moment neither they nor I will ever forget.

Figure 5.3   Making Expert Connections

CHALLENGING INVESTIGATION	POSSIBLE EXPERT CONNECTION THAT DOES NOT REQUIRE FACE-TO-FACE INTERACTION
How can we influence current legislation regarding the proposed gaming resorts slated for possible construction in the upcoming year?	Students write proposed legislation and send it to the appropriate state congressional member. This could be done via e-mail or snail mail.
How can we write a series of children's books to teach a moral lesson?	Students write and print books using an online publisher to be sent to a children's home or youth home in the community. Students could first send their drafts of the stories using Google Drive to a local community college professor for editing.
How can we help to stop the proposed elimination of the family consumer science department at our school?	Students can use Prezi to create online presentations to send to the school board for review.
How can we create a marketing plan for a local small business?	Students create the marketing plan and submit the proposals to the appropriate business leaders via online tools or as hard copy through the mail.

Note: These Challenging Investigations could be adapted for the appropriate grade level, and experts listed are suggestions only. Depending on available resources and numbers of students, modifications may need to be made.

Using Technology to Connect to Your Audience

With the technology that many districts have readily available, it is possible to virtually connect to the world beyond the classroom. Skype is an easy-to-use and free tool for making expert connections. Other videoconferencing equipment can be utilized as well. I've used Skype in a variety of ways: to connect my students to soldiers serving in Afghanistan, a U.S. federal court justice, and several descendants of those involved in the *Brown v. Board of*

Education case, to name a few. Skype helps you overcome the logistical issues of travel and potential costs involved. Thus, presentations can be made via Skype or final products can be sent via other Web 2.0 tools (see Figure 5.4), and feedback with the expert could then take place via Skype.

Figure 5.4   Web 2.0 Tools to Connect to an Outside Audience

WEB 2.0 TOOL	POSSIBLE USE #1	POSSIBLE USE #2
Skype	Connect with an expert who can't travel to your location due to cost or logistical constraints.	Present to a wider audience, such as a legislative meeting, to have the voices of your students heard.
VoiceThread	In a foreign language class, have students use VoiceThread and have native speakers leave comments as feedback.	Upload created artwork to VoiceThread and ask an artist to provide comments as feedback.
Twitter	Conduct a Twitter chat using a specific hashtag in which you engage your students with experts and peers from around the globe.	Post links to student work and solicit input from your Twitter followers. Ask for comments on blogs, websites, or Prezis.
Museum Box	Create an online exhibit depicting a particular era in history in your community. Submit the exhibit for review by members of the local historical society.	Create an online exhibit that reflects and extends an oral history project. Have the subject of the oral history review the exhibit.
Wix	Create a website for a local community organization.	Create a website to submit as an entry for a national or international competition.
TodaysMeet	Organize an online presentation to a group of experts located in another state.	Organize an online presentation for an international group that your students have partnered with to work on solving a global issue.

Note: Please use caution when posting student work online. Follow the guidelines made and enforced by your district, and review digital citizenship rules with your students. Check out other Web 2.0 tools at cooltoolsforschools.wikispaces.com.

Utilizing technology does have its caveats. Obviously, we have to be ever vigilant of the threats that unmonitored and unregulated Internet interaction can produce. However, that aside, simply posting student work on the Internet via a blog or as a video showcase doesn't produce the desired results of the outside audience element. Without thoughtful and intentional integration of technology, we fall into the trap of merely hoping our students' work will be viewed. Thus, ensure you have a target audience. Make connections with experts online, and ask for their feedback contributions. There are several great organizations that already are set up to provide feedback to your students (see Figure 5.5 below). English and social studies teachers might want to check out the Harlan Institute and their online FantasySCOTUS program. Students blog about their predictions for upcoming U.S. Supreme Court cases to earn badges and receive feedback from legal professionals. One World Education out of Washington, D.C., is another model online program in which students write about their ideas, values, and perspectives, and units are created solely around student writing. In addition to organizations, you may also want to check out several online sponsored competitions. GlobalSchoolNet.org sponsors two such competitions: The International CyberFair focuses on elementary through secondary grade levels and all subject areas, and Doors to Diplomacy, cosponsored by the U.S. State Department, targets social studies, science, art, and English students from around the world at the high school level. The Real World Design Challenge gives high school students the opportunity to tackle "real problems" with "real tools" as they take on "real roles" and create "real contributions" in team engineering challenges (http://www.globalschoolnet.org/gsncf).

Figure 5.5 Competitions That Already Have an Outside Audience

- FantasySCOTUS. . . . . .www.fantasyscotus.net
- One World Education . . . . .www.oneworldeducation.org
- International CyberFair. . . . . .www.globalschoolnet.org/gsncf/aglance.cfm
- Doors to Diplomacy . . . . .www.globalschoolnet.org/gsndoors/index.cfm
- Real World Design Challenge . . . . .www.realworlddesignchallenge.org

The Outside Audience Promotes the Justification Element

Using an outside audience is not only a means to have students produce professional work, but it is also a means to ensure the students are implementing the justification phase of the Authentic Learning Experience. If students are going to have an audience that reaches beyond the classroom walls and beyond the ears of the teacher and student peers, they are going to have to think critically about the content that is at the heart of the challenging investigation. Since the challenging investigation is open-ended to allow for a variety of solutions and the goal is to justify the end product, students must walk their audience through this justification phase. The goal is to have the audience engage with the students and question their solution. Therefore, it becomes necessary to prep your audience with this request. The more the audience engages with the students, the better you will be able to assess the students' understanding of the content and their critical-thinking process. You could provide your audience with a simplified rubric or a checklist with the targeted areas for assessment. Have the audience provide your students with feedback, either verbally or in writing. However, assessments that are made by your audience should never be part of students' grades. Remember, while the audience may be the professional experts in the field of study, you are still the expert when it comes to knowing and assessing your students! (To learn more about assessing student work, see Chapter 8.)

If this chapter has left you feeling overwhelmed or, better yet, inspired, read some of the following detailed examples to get a better look at implementing the outside audience in a truly authentic manner.

Sample Authentic Learning Experiences

Murals of York

Amy Musone
Roundtown Elementary School
York, Pennsylvania

School Background

The Central York School District is a suburban district with a population of nearly 6,000 students. The community is socioeconomically and racially diverse; 20 percent of students are minorities. The district is heavily invested in technology use for all students and provides a great deal of teacher training in technology integration. However, the district is not currently implementing a one-to-one program.

Challenging Investigation

How can we help preserve the history of York?

Authentic Learning Experience Description

It all began with the annual third-grade field trip to the York Agriculture and Industrial Museum and mural walk. In a personal effort to learn more about the eighteen murals that are painted in a variety of locations in the city of York, depicting the history of the community since the 1700s, teacher Amy Musone discovered that the murals were meant to last only approximately twenty years. With the realization that many of these murals would not be preserved for the future children of her students, the challenging investigation was born and spanned over the course of four years, each year building on the previous work of students.

In a true community connection, students worked with local historians from the York County Heritage Trust and local mural artists to research the historical events depicted in the murals and how the murals were created. The first year students involved in this Authentic Learning Experience produced a website showcasing the murals. The website included pictures of the murals taken by the students, as well as a Google Map tour of the murals. Informative written descriptions and accompanying videos were created and linked to the York County Heritage Trust website in order to truly have an outside audience. However, all information included in the website design was approved by the York County Heritage Trust, as students had to go through the justification process before their work would be accepted.

In an effort to expand the project into a second year, students again worked with local historians to increase their knowledge about the murals. The goal of continued collaboration and research led to the discovery that no Wikipedia article on the murals existed. Thus, the final product reached an even wider outside audience, as the students wrote, submitted, and had accepted an article for publication on Wikipedia. The process for submitting and publishing an article to Wikipedia includes intense justification of all information contained within the article.

In the third year of the project, the students once again worked with historians and mural artists to build their background knowledge of the murals and the historical importance of the city of York. This time, however, they really tapped into their artistic sides and focused on creating a tie between social studies and art. Students worked directly with one of the York mural artists to create their own murals that represented the history of their elementary school, drawing on an even closer community connection for the students. The canvas murals served as an oral history of the school, both past and present. The canvases were donated and put on display at the school library and at the York County Heritage Trust, as an extension of the outside audience element.

At the time of this writing, the project was entering the fourth year of extended implementation. The plan is to include individual student choice of a York business or manufacturer on which to do a detailed research study through interviews and historical record reviews. Students will be tasked with creating a lasting artifact to tell the story of the business and will once again partner with the York County Heritage Trust for the display of the artifacts.

COMMON CORE STATE STANDARDS

3.RIT.3	Describe the relationship between a series of historical events, scientific ideas or concepts, or steps in technical procedures in a text, using language that pertains to time, sequence, and cause/effect.
3.RIT.10	Read and comprehend informational texts, including history/social studies, science, and technical texts … independently and proficiently.
3.W.2	Write informative/explanatory texts to examine a topic and convey ideas and information clearly.

3.W.4	With guidance and support from adults, produce writing in which the development and organization are appropriate to task and purpose.
3.W.5	With guidance and support from peers and adults, develop and strengthen writing as needed by planning, revising, and editing.
3.W.6	With guidance and support from adults, use technology to produce and publish writing as well as to interact and collaborate with others.
3.W.8	Recall information from experiences or gather information from print and digital sources; take brief notes on sources and sort evidence into provided categories.
3. SL.3	Ask and answer questions about information from a speaker, offering appropriate elaboration and detail.

Technology Integration

Students were introduced to a variety of technology tools throughout the multiyear process. While technology is a focus for this district, Google Maps and Livescribe pens were new to students, and they were an integral part of the experience. The Livescribe pens allowed students to record interviewed material, and Google Maps helped students to locate the various works of art in the city. Students also used Google Drive to foster their collaborative writing with their peers, their high school reviewers, and their teacher.

Teacher Reflection

"As I think back upon the process, I am touched by how willing people were to give their time and their expertise to create engaging, relevant learning experiences for my students. I am not an expert on local history, or art, or even knowing where to locate some of the resources my students needed. The collaboration that occurred was so much more than I could have imagined, both on the adult end and student end. Students became experts and taught each other along the way. Even students from years past taught students of present through their digital artifacts."—Amy Musone

Power Plant Efficiency

Kristyn Kamps
Holland Christian Middle School
Holland, Michigan

School Background
Holland Christian Schools are private, Christian faith–based schools that place a high value on academic excellence and the development of 21st-century skills through community partnerships and technology integration.

Challenging Investigation
How can the city of Holland produce power more efficiently and still meet the demand for power usage?

Authentic Learning Experience Description
The inception for this Authentic Learning Experience came after students read an article about a neighboring state's power plant that had an efficiency rating of 33 percent, meaning that 67 percent of the potential energy stored in the coal that is used to create electricity is lost. Based on these dismal findings, the challenging investigation was created, as students were concerned their own local power plant might rate in a similar efficiency category. The investigation required students to best meet the needs of the community while considering the plant's capacity, output, size, and operating budget.

    Throughout the processes, a great deal of care was taken to scaffold the concepts for the students. An activity in which the students had to create their own imaginary community and determine the best method of energy production was supported by a variety of steps. In fact, a parent volunteer and owner of a local construction company created a scale model of an island for student use in the community design. This enabled the students to visualize the 3-D concept of the island rather than simply having to rely on the use of topographical maps. Additionally, students visited the local power plant and then researched ways communities around the world produce power. These included biomass energy in Hawaii, geothermal power in Iceland, wind energy in the Netherlands, and tidal energy in France. Students also investigated ways coal-burning plants had increased their efficiency around the country and world. Students communicated with university professors and officials from the researched areas around the world to get firsthand knowledge of the methodologies they were considering for their own community. In fact, the students initiated the communication themselves. They explored the potential contacts and sent e-mail inquiries to the chosen professionals. The research from around the world was made more meaningful for the students, as there was a clear community connection for the students in the application of their learning to improving the energy situation in their own hometown.

Student teams used their research to create a justification for their solution to the challenging investigation. During this process, students had to create graphs of past energy consumption based on data from the power plant and, using the trends from the past, predict what energy needs would be in the future. Thus, students were looking at not only the trends in population growth but also how energy production might change the need of the population as they potentially started using energy-saving measures such as compact fluorescent lightbulbs. The research, solutions, and presentation were made even more powerful as the teams from two science classes debated each possible solution created to determine which overall solution was presented to an outside audience, the supervisor of Holland's power plant. Interestingly enough, one student proposal was very similar to what was already being considered by the operators of the plant.

COMMON CORE STATE STANDARDS

8.RIT.1	Cite the textual evidence that most strongly supports an analysis of what the text says explicitly as well as inferences drawn from the text.
8.RIT.3	Analyze how a text makes connections among and distinctions between individuals, ideas, or events (e.g., through comparisons, analogies, or categories).
8.RIT.8	Delineate and evaluate the argument and specific claims in a text, assessing whether the reasoning is sound and the evidence is relevant and sufficient; recognize when irrelevant evidence is introduced.
8.W.1	Write arguments to support claims with clear reasons and relevant evidence.
8.W.7	Conduct short research projects to answer a question (including a self-generated question), drawing on several sources and generating additional related, focused questions that allow for multiple avenues of exploration.

8.W.9	Draw evidence from literary or informational texts to support analysis, reflection, and research.
8.SL.4	Present claims and findings, emphasizing salient points in a focused, coherent manner with relevant evidence, sound valid reasoning, and well-chosen details; use appropriate eye contact, adequate volume, and clear pronunciation.
8.G.9	Know the formulas for the volumes of cones, cylinders, and spheres and use them to solve real-world and mathematical problems.
8.F.4	Construct a function to model a linear relationship between two quantities. Determine the rate of change and initial value of the function from a description of a relationship or from two (x, y) values, including reading these from a table or from a graph. Interpret the rate of change and initial value of a linear function in terms of the situation it models, and in terms of its graph or a table of values.
8.F.5	Describe quantitatively the functional relationship between two quantities by analyzing a graph. Sketch a graph that exhibits the qualitative features of a function that has been described verbally.

Technology Integration

Students used spreadsheets, PowerPoint, and Google SketchUp to complete this Authentic Learning Experience. Technology was incorporated as an "invisible tool," according to Kristyn Kamps, so that the focus was on the content and critical-thinking skills, rather than the incorporation of the technology.

Teacher Reflection

"This investigation started out as a research project, but because of student interest and our ability to pull in experts from around the world, it became this engaging, extended learning experience that encompassed science, math, and technology. We spent time with experts at our local power plant who invested in the project and assisted us in creating quality presentations that were accurate and impressive. Dave Koster, the former head of the power plant, continues to speak highly of the work my students accomplished with his help and the help of his colleagues. It was an experience that took time and intentional planning to pull together; however, the passion it produced in my students was well worth it!"
—Kristyn Kamps

Nonverbal Communication Etiquette (NVCE)

Tamara Seymour
Mexico High School
Mexico, New York

School Background
Mexico High School services nearly 750 students, with approximately half of
the students qualifying for free or reduced-cost lunch. Students are required to
complete community service hours in order to gain a "sense of connection with the
surrounding community" and to "give back to the community."

Challenging Investigation
How can we improve communication between local businesses in our town and
deaf, hard-of-hearing, or speech-impaired (DHHSI) customers?

Authentic Learning Experience Description
Students on Tamara Seymour's caseload know what it means to have difficulty
communicating with others in public. Experiencing this on a daily basis fueled their
desire to solve the challenging investigation. A natural community connection
existed, as these students wanted to improve their ability to communicate with
local businesses they patronize and knew they had to help the businesses to
achieve this desire.

Students interviewed employees, managers, and owners of approximately forty
area businesses to determine ways that they were currently serving the DHHSI
population. This was no easy task for students who live with these disabilities,
and as they documented the process, they learned there was a definite need for
NVCE at these businesses. In response to this need, students determined they had
to take several steps to encourage NVCE. Students created a brochure of NVCE to
explain the different methods of alternate communication and the importance
of always maintaining eye contact, speaking clearly, and speaking at a normal
speed. The brochure also examined common myths that are associated with
communicating with DHHSI individuals. In addition, the students created a DVD

in which they modeled both correct and incorrect communication methods with DHHSI customers. The students packaged a kit that included these products, as well as a laminated question mark to be prominently located near a cash register in order to enable a DHHSI customer to discretely point to it if additional assistance is needed. Also, a notepad and pencil bearing a student-created logo with the American Sign Language symbol for "I love you" were packaged. These kits were distributed to the local businesses at a presentation of the students' learning, in which the students had no trouble providing a justification for their learning for this outside audience. In fact, the students reported in their personal reflections that they really appreciated learning how to talk with the business leaders in order to gain confidence in their own communication abilities.

COMMON CORE STATE STANDARDS

11.RIT.7	Integrate and evaluate multiple sources of information presented in different media or formats as well as in words in order to address a question or solve a problem.
11.W.2	Write informative/explanatory texts to examine and convey complex ideas, concepts, and information clearly and accurately through the effective selection, organization, and analysis of content.
11.W.4	Produce clear and coherent writing in which the development, organization, and style are appropriate to task, purpose, and audience.
11.W.5	Develop and strengthen writing as needed by planning, revising, editing, rewriting, or trying a new approach, focusing on addressing what is most significant for a specific purpose and audience.
11.W.7	Conduct short as well as more sustained research projects to answer a question (including a self-generated question) or solve a problem; narrow or broaden the inquiry when appropriate; synthesize multiple sources on the subject, demonstrating understanding of the subject under investigation.
11.SL.4	Present information, findings, and supporting evidence, conveying a clear and distinct perspective, such that listeners can follow the line of reasoning, alternative or opposing perspectives are addressed, and the organization, development, substance, and style are appropriate to purpose, audience, and a range of formal and informal tasks.

Technology Integration

Students used Flip cameras to record their videos and used Movie Maker. Students were empowered with these technology devices to meet their own needs, as well as to use them to inform others about their disabilities.

Teacher Reflection

"This was meaningful to my students. All of the students had experienced communication hiccups when frequenting businesses, so they were eager to participate in hopes of 'making a difference.' It was amazing to witness students' confidence and communication skills strengthen as we revisited businesses for different phases of our project. The students learned their strengths and supported one another. Everyone shared a speaking role in our final public presentation. The tie-in to the community was valuable in making the project meaningful for the students. The feedback from parents, staff, and businesses was supportive and encouraging. Many businesses welcomed the training and education we provided. As we revisited some of the businesses, we witnessed 'change,' such as seeing our question mark next to the cash register. It was a positive learning experience for everyone."—Tamara Seymour

CHAPTER 6

—— ■ ——

The Common Core and Other State Standards

As of the printing of this book, forty-five states and four territories have adopted the Common Core State Standards. Even if you are not an educator directly affected by the Common Core, you should still be interested in this chapter, as standards, no matter how or by whom they are written, should be a foundation for Authentic Learning Experiences. Additionally, regardless of what your thoughts may be about a "nationally created curriculum" (as some critics call the Common Core), there is no denying that upon further study, the Common Core is fundamentally about raising the expectations for students in preparation for both college and career demands in this era.

The development of the Common Core came about in an effort to level the requirements that students should achieve no matter in which district, community, or state they live. It is understandable that not all states would be enthusiastic about pledging to join with the implementation process. After all, constitutionally, educational decisions should be left up to the states. However, it must be noted that, according to the Common Core State Standards Initiative, the Common Core development is a direct result of a partnership between parents, teachers, and school officials from the Council of Chief State School Officers and the National Governors Association Center for Best Practices. Many teacher organizations such as the National Education Association and the National Council of Teachers of English provided feedback during the creation of the Common Core State Standards. Additionally, in an effort to maintain state control, states are allowed to add up to 15 percent additional material to the standards (Common Core State Standards Initiative, 2010).

It was logical, in the wake of No Child Left Behind and the various ways in which this act was implemented, that a national standard be set in order to ensure all students are adequately prepared when they leave our public (and private) schools. Through NCLB, states determined the achievement standards for their students. Thus, the reasonable next step to ensure students are in fact achieving an equitable education is to provide the standards they should be taught. Simply put, I find the Common Core State Standards to be more of a guiding framework for educators who are striving to improve and hone their own teaching skill set. A closer analysis of the mission statement on the home page of the Common Core website supports this. "The Common Core State Standards provide a consistent, clear understanding of what students are expected to learn, so teachers and parents know what they need to do to help them. The standards are designed to be robust and relevant to the real world, reflecting the knowledge and skills that our young people need for success in college and careers" (Common Core State Standards Initiative, 2010). Every facet of this mission statement supports the guiding principles of the Authentic Learning Experiences framework.

Testing in the Common Core Era

Two major testing associations have formed in response to the Common Core. The Partnership for Assessment of Readiness for College and Careers (PARCC) and the Smarter Balanced Assessment Consortium (SBAC) are designing assessments that measure student progress and can be used to inform instruction (see Figure 6.1, page 101). Using the data from midyear or interim assessments will guide teachers to standards that need to be reinforced or, in some cases, retaught in order to best prepare all students for the college and career readiness stance that the Common Core State Standards espouse. However, through the careful construction and implementation of Authentic Learning Experiences, grade-level standards are easily included in the everyday curricular implementation process.

> ✓ **Check for Understanding**
> Review the sample test items from either PARCC or SBAC. Create a list of possible Authentic Learning Experiences linked to a minimum of three sample test items. Share and discuss your determinations at your next department meeting or curriculum workday.

Incorporating classroom experiences that promote critical thinking is imperative in preparing students to take standardized tests, and the tests being developed by both PARCC and SBAC are no exception. An analysis of a variety of questions from these tests reveals a focus on higher-order thinking skills. Students are required to apply knowledge gained through the implementation of the Common Core State Standards in relation to the course content. Additionally, students evaluate and analyze literature, non-fiction text, and mathematical problems. Both PARCC and SBAC have released sample test questions for review. An example problem from the ELA/literacy SBAC sample test requires students in the grade 3–5 band to revise a given paragraph by adding details from a particular daily school schedule that help support reasons for having a longer school day. This model problem could easily be designed into an Authentic Learning Experience in which students present solutions to a challenging investigation of a similar nature to the school board. Similarly, an example math problem from the PARCC sample test requires fourth-grade students to determine the greatest number of seats that could fit into a baseball stadium. This, too, could be developed into an Authentic Learning Experience where students are given a challenging investigation that requires them to design a new baseball stadium for their city that will attract investors, increase attendees, and receive the support of the city commissioners. This type of an investigation would be well suited for a school located in a smaller city that has been considering the possibility of attracting a minor-league team. Additionally, the type of venue could be changed from a baseball stadium to any other possible need for the school or community but still include the requirement of determining seating capacity.

Figure 6.1   Common Core Testing Websites

- PARCC: . . . . .www.parcconline.org
- SBAC: . . . . www.smarterbalanced.org

Directly Connecting the Elements of Authentic Learning Experiences to the Test

As discussed in the previous chapters on designing Authentic Learning Experiences, the key elements of the experiences promote critical thinking, communication, collaboration, and the ability to make connections to the world in which we live. After further review of the Common Core testing materials, it is evident that each of the four elements is directly tied to the performance of students at a proficient and advanced level. Figure 6.2 (below) shows the links between the elements of Authentic Learning Experiences and SBAC's major content categories.

The designed "performance tasks" of the SBAC test are extended reviews of student learning that take place in the classroom over the course of approximately a week. These tasks, too, are directly aligned with Authentic Learning Experiences. For instance, the sample eleventh-grade performance task, "Nuclear Power: Friend or Foe?," requires students to "conduct research on the pros and cons of nuclear power and then write a report arguing your opinion on the use of nuclear power for generating electricity." This performance task could be extended into an Authentic Learning Experience for students who live near a nuclear power plant. My students, who live just outside of the ten-mile radius of Three Mile Island, could engage in similar research. The challenging investigation could take a variety of angles depending on the course in which it would be implemented. Students could focus on proposing ways to make the emergency response system to a nuclear disaster more effective or could create arguments for why Unit 2, which was damaged in the 1979 accident, should be reopened in order to produce needed power. Depending on the focus of the experience, students could submit their findings to either the U.S. Nuclear Regulatory Commission or the Exelon managers who run the plant.

Figure 6.2   How the Elements of Authentic Learning Experiences Connect to SBAC

ELEMENTS OF AUTHENTIC LEARNING EXPERIENCES	SBAC LITERACY CLAIMS	SBAC MATH CLAIMS
Challenging Investigation	"Students can engage in research and inquiry to investigate topics, and to analyze, integrate, and present information."	"Students can solve a range of complex, well-posed problems in pure and applied mathematics, making productive use of knowledge and problem solving strategies."
Community/ Career Connection	"Students can read closely and analytically to comprehend a range of increasingly complex literary and informational texts."	"Students can analyze complex, real-world scenarios and can construct and use mathematical models to interpret and solve problems."
Justification	"Students can read closely and analytically to comprehend a range of increasingly complex literary and informational texts."	"Students can clearly and precisely construct viable arguments to support their own reasoning and to critique the reasoning of others."

ELEMENTS OF AUTHENTIC LEARNING EXPERIENCES	SBAC LITERACY CLAIMS	SBAC MATH CLAIMS
Outside Audience	"Students can produce effective and well-grounded writing for a range of purposes and audiences." "Students can employ effective speaking and listening skills for a range of purposes and audiences."	"Students can explain and apply mathematical concepts and interpret and carry out mathematical procedures with precision and fluency."

Note: Content claims are the major categories for looking at student performance.

Sources: "Claims for the English Language Arts/Literacy/Summative Assessment," 2012, March 1; "Claims for the Mathematics Summative Assessment," 2012, May 8.

In the previous design chapters on Authentic Learning Experiences, each example provided showcases the Common Core State Standards addressed. In all honesty, many of the teachers designed these experiences without the Common Core State Standards in mind. I read about the experiences, interviewed the teachers, and matched the standards to each experience.

My honesty about this is in an effort to assure you of two things. First and foremost, if you create an Authentic Learning Experience following the four design principles, you will inevitably be incorporating Common Core State Standards. Now, that isn't to say the standards aren't important. They most definitely are important. However, I do believe that the standards help to provide the reason it is necessary to create Authentic Learning Experiences. We, as educators, have to begin to intentionally focus on these standards, which leads me to the second reason behind my honesty. Not every educator who reads this book will be concerned about the Common Core State Standards. Perhaps the state where you teach has chosen not to adopt the standards, but you are still bound to prepare your students for either the collegiate or career world beyond the classroom. Authentic Learning Experiences create an atmosphere ripe for this preparation. The Common Core State Standards are simply a support to these experiences.

Note the variety of standards listed in each of the example Authentic Learning Experiences provided throughout this book. Notice how a science example not only includes math standards but also English language arts standards. Focus on how an art example incorporates both sets of standards as well. While not every example provided includes both the math and ELA components, many do. This serves as a reminder that no matter what content area we teach, we can and should find ways to naturally include math and ELA into our Authentic Learning Experiences.

Sample Authentic Learning Experiences

Rain Garden

Erin McMahon
Monocacy Elementary School
Frederick, Maryland

School Background

Monocacy Elementary is located in the heart of the city of Frederick. The school, with a population of just more than 700, provides full Title I services to its students. More than 50 percent of the students qualify for free or reduced-cost meals, as this school educates the highest number of homeless students in the Frederick County Public Schools. Additionally, 27 different languages are spoken at Monocacy, and it has become the English language learner magnet school in the district.

Challenging Investigation

How can we help to eliminate the pollutants seeping into our schoolyard?

Authentic Learning Experience Description

Erin McMahon has always believed her students should experience learning organically. Student interests and concerns typically drive the design of her classroom focus, and the creation of this Authentic Learning Experience was no exception. After a hard rain, McMahon's students noticed "yucky stuff" floating on the top of the water that pooled in a drainage area next to the school. The students' natural curiosity prompted them to ask questions about the composition of this "yucky stuff," and the students effectively created their own challenging investigation. The relationship of the investigation to the school and local area provided students with a community connection that truly made the students passionate about the experience. Through the students' investigation, the determination was made that the neighboring parking lot with parked vehicles was the cause of the pollutants that were pooling in the area after a hard rain. Students researched the causes of these pollutants and ways in which they could effectively lessen the impact of these pollutants.

Students' research ultimately focused on rain gardens, and the students determined that they needed to create a rain garden for their school. Students gathered data and collected research to support their cause. Students then decided which native plants to incorporate into their garden. They had to calculate the costs for these plants and integrate the math to design the garden. In the justification phase of the experience, because of the need for funding and support for this project, the students had to seek approval and secure funds to make their vision become a reality. The students presented their findings to an outside audience that consisted of the school administrators as well as the school PTA. Ultimately, students desired to encourage other areas in their county to plant rain gardens and, consequently, chose an additional outside audience. Students wrote persuasive essays they sent to the district's middle school to encourage the planting of a rain garden in order to protect a stream near the school. Additionally, one student took her audience even further and wrote a letter to the editor at the local paper to report on the findings of the classroom.

COMMON CORE STATE STANDARDS

5.RIT.4	Determine the meaning of general academic and domain-specific words and phrases in a text relevant to a grade 5 topic or subject area.
5.RIT.5	Compare and contrast the overall structure of events, ideas, concepts, or information in two or more texts.
5. RIT. 7	Draw on information from multiple print or digital sources, demonstrating the ability to locate an answer to a question quickly or to solve a problem efficiently.
5.RIT.9	Integrate information from several texts on the same topic in order to write or speak about the subject knowledgeably.
5.RFS.4	Read with sufficient accuracy and fluency to support comprehension.
5.W.1	Write opinion pieces on topics or texts, supporting a point of view with reasons and information.
5.W.4	Produce clear and coherent writing in which the development and organization are appropriate to task, purpose, and audience.
5.W.9	Draw evidence from literary or informational texts to support analysis, reflection, and research.
5.SL.4	Report on a topic or text or present an opinion, sequencing ideas logically and using appropriate facts and relevant, descriptive details to support main ideas or themes; speak clearly at an understandable pace.
5.SL.5	Include multimedia components and visual displays in presentations when appropriate to enhance the development of main ideas or themes.

5.NBT.3	Read, write, and compare decimals to thousandths.
5.NBT.4	Use place value understanding to round decimals to any place.
5.MD.1	Convert among different-sized standard measurement units within a given measurement system, and use these conversions in solving multi-step, real world problems.
5.G.3	Understand that attributes belonging to a category of two-dimensional figures also belong to all subcategories of that category.

Technology Integration

Students utilized the Internet to conduct their research on pollution and the rain gardens. For the presentation proposal that was given to administration, the students created PowerPoint slides to enhance the visual appeal of the presentation.

Teacher Reflection

"As an educator, it has always been my goal to teach students the content they will need to know to be successful, but through the implementation of this experience, I have seen that content come to life. Allowing students to have an active role in their education by letting their curious nature to bring content into application has not only given me a new perspective into how I can teach and students can learn, but also how students can impact the world around them. I can't think of a more meaningful way to teach math, reading, writing, research, social studies, science, and technology skills than through real-life application and student inquiry during this rain garden experience. Based upon student observation and concern, not only did the students use content to find a solution to the problem occurring in their school yard, but they also created community awareness about pollution and offered solutions for how it can be stopped. The success of this project was immeasurable due to the fact that my students not only learned content and put content into action, but most importantly made their voices heard and left a positive mark on their community, in their school yard, and on their stream. They now have ownership of their rain garden and have been given the charge to educate others about the importance of rain gardens and ways to lessen pollutants in our environment . . . which is the most successful [lesson] of all."—Erin McMahon

Global Reforestation

Amy Schmer, Tracey Winey, and Alana Fournet
Preston Middle School/Little Children of the Philippines
Fort Collins, Colorado/Dumaguete, Philippines

School Background

Preston Middle School is a suburban STEM school in the Poudre School District that services sixth through eighth grades. The teachers and administration at Preston believe that all students deserve the opportunity to become STEM confident and competent learners. The school routinely integrates Authentic Learning Experiences and has connected its 1,000 plus students to a variety of experts and community partnerships over the last several years.

Little Children of the Philippines (LCP) is an orphanage that provides shelter, food, health services, and education to many youths in need.

Challenging Investigation

How can we help to decrease the effects of deforestation in the Philippines?

Authentic Learning Experience Description

Preston Middle School and Little Children of the Philippines first connected in 2009 through a former Preston teacher, Alana Fournet, who had moved to the Philippines as a Peace Corps volunteer and worked at LCP. The students met one another through live video chats on a number of occasions. Preston's building-wide literacy initiative led to the establishment of a virtual book club in 2010 between the U.S. and Filipino students. Both sets of students read the same book, e-mailed questions, and discussed their thoughts about their reading reflections with one another. In addition, video chats continued, and at the conclusion of the virtual book club, students reflected on their cultural understanding of one another. Some students began a traditional pen-pal correspondence.

In 2011, Typhoon Sendong struck the Philippines. Many lives were tragically lost, and one hillside of the LCP campus was devastated. Around the same time, Amy Schmer and Tracey Winey had assembled a new class with motivated, STEM-centric students. The theme of this class was completely student driven, with the guiding principle that the students pick a global problem to solve. The Preston students generated many ideas and ultimately chose inviting the students from LCP to collaborate on decreasing deforestation in the Philippines. Thus, they took true ownership of the challenging investigation as well as created a clear global community connection.

Without a solid background in deforestation, the teachers turned to David Neils, founder of the International Telementor Program (www.telementor.org), to locate and connect students with individual expert mentors. Within twenty-four hours, each student, both in the U.S. and the Philippines, had an expert mentor in the forestation field who spoke his or her own language. This connection proved invaluable for research and also for guidance as the students worked through the justification phase of the experience. Students wrote twice a week to their mentors to provide explanations of their work, ask for additional support, and synthesize their findings.

The students on both sides researched causes of deforestation in depth. They shared their learning with one another through PowerPoint, e-mails, and video chats. After gaining an understanding of the political, economical, and social reasons for deforestation, the students started collaborating on possible viable solutions. Students shared their ideas with one another, their mentors, and their teachers. This outside audience gave feedback, and the students further developed solutions.

Through the ongoing virtual chats between the two groups of students, the Filipino students taught the Preston students about how they cooked food and lit their houses. Some of these basic heating methods contributed to the deforestation problem and had other negative effects, such as smoke inhalation. It was through these discussions that students decided to focus their efforts on implementing more efficient and less environmentally destructive methods of heating and cooking in the Filipino homes. Thus, students on both sides of the ocean investigated different possibilities for heating and cooking that would be less reliant on wood, directly helping to decrease the deforestation taking place in the Philippines. Students researched different types of biomass stoves and compared how much wood each mechanism used. Students at Preston partnered with a Colorado State University engineering student who brought different biomass stoves for the Preston students to test and compare. This portion of the experience helped students in the justification phase of their experience.

Ultimately, through Alana Fournet's leadership and the support of the students' mentors, an education camp was offered for more than 100 Philippine students. The Philippine Army provided transportation to and from the camp, and students traveled several hours to the camp. Students learned more about teamwork, causes of deforestation, and how to use biomass stoves. Each student was given a biomass stove to take home to his or her family. Preston and LCP students hope the education about and the acquisition of the stoves will dramatically reduce deforestation.

At home in Fort Collins, the Preston students reached another outside audience as they taught community members about this unique opportunity to give back to the global community. The list of guests included the scientists, college professors, and master gardeners who had helped the students throughout their learning, as well as state representatives, community members, and parents. The Preston students educated their listeners on causes of deforestation, reforestation, working together, and the joys of learning and befriending youths on the other side of the world.

COMMON CORE STATE STANDARDS

6.RIT.1	Cite textual evidence to support analysis of what the text says explicitly as well as inferences drawn from the text.
6.RIT.4	Determine the meaning of words and phrases as they are used in a text, including figurative, connotative, and technical meanings.
6.RIT.7	Integrate information presented in different media or formats as well as in words to develop a coherent understanding of a topic or issue.
6.RIT.8	Trace and evaluate the argument and specific claims in a text, distinguishing claims that are supported by reasons and evidence from claims that are not.
6.W.2	Write informative/explanatory texts to examine a topic and convey ideas, concepts, and information through the selection, organization, and analysis of relevant content.
6.W.4	Produce clear and coherent writing in which the development, organization, and style are appropriate to task, purpose, and audience.
6.W.5	With some guidance and support from peers and adults, develop and strengthen writing as needed by planning, revising, editing, rewriting, or trying a new approach.
6.W.7	Conduct short research projects to answer a question, drawing on several sources and refocusing the inquiry when appropriate.
6.W.9	Draw evidence from literary or informational texts to support analysis, reflection, and research.
6.SL.1	Engage effectively in a range of collaborative discussions with diverse partners of grade 6 topics, texts, and issues, building on others' ideas and expressing their own clearly.

6.SL.3	Delineate a speaker's argument and specific claims, distinguishing claims that are supported by reasons and evidence from claims that are not.
6.SL.4	Present claims and findings, sequencing ideas logically and using pertinent descriptions, facts, and details to accentuate main ideas or themes; use appropriate eye contact, adequate volume, and clear pronunciation.
6.EE.6	Use variables to represent numbers and write expressions when solving a real-world or mathematical problem; understand that a variable can represent an unknown number, or, depending on the purpose at hand, any number in a specified set.
6.EE.7	Solve real-world and mathematical problems by writing and solving equations of the form $x + p = q$ and $px + q$ for cases in which p, q, and x are all nonnegative rational numbers.
6.EE.9	Use variables to represent two quantities in a real-world problem that change in relationship to one another; write an equation to express one quantity, thought of as the dependent variable, in terms of the other quantity, thought of as the independent variable. Analyze the relationship between the dependent and independent variables using graphs and tables, and relate these to the equation.
6.SP.1	Recognize a statistical question as one that anticipates variability in the data related to the question and accounts for it in the answers.
6.SP.5	Summarize numerical data sets in relation to their context.

Technology Integration

As this was an experience that connected two countries across the globe from each other, students connected via videos made with Movie Maker and iMovie and uploaded to YouTube. Students also used WebEx to conduct online conferencing.

Teacher Reflection

"Regardless of who the students are, we believe that all children have the capability to solve real-world problems. We, as the teachers, learn right alongside the students, and we are only there to help facilitate when the students get stuck or need someone to ask some questions that they may not have thought about. Our classes are truly student centered. The teachers do not drive the class; the kids do. When they need to slow down, we do. When they are ready to move fast, we move fast. This type of class is so powerful! Middle school students can impact the world today; we just need to give them the opportunity to show us."—Amy Schmer and Tracy Winey

IChallengeU

Jason Pasatta (Program Coordinator)
Ottawa Area Intermediate School District
Holland, Michigan

School Background

Students were drawn from the fourteen area high schools in Ottawa County. These schools represent a diverse population and include both general education and career/technical education schools.

Challenging Investigation

The Challenging Investigation varied, as it was dependent on the community or business partnership assignment.

Authentic Learning Experience Description

This two-week summer program was designed to connect area high school students with corporate, community, and civic leaders. Both students and teachers in the program were chosen based on an application and interview selection process. Teachers underwent training for the program and connected with their community liaisons to develop challenging investigations for the students to explore. These questions ranged in scope based on the community or corporate connection. Some of the investigations explored included these: "How can we make the Haworth Inn & Conference Center a more desirable place for booking special events?" and "How can the United Way successfully distribute healthy meals to families in need in Ottawa County?" (Note: The food was available, but the effective distribution of the food was a problem.) The goals of the program focused on the community/career connection as they included building the 21st-century skills of the students, introducing students to possible career pathways, and building a strong association between the schools and the community partnerships involved. Additionally, the teachers who participated in this summer program were anxious to take these types of Authentic Learning Experiences back into the classroom for further development. Zeeland East High School science teacher Mike Fenlon reflected on his own professional learning from the program: "My involvement in the IChallengeU program has allowed me to access materials and do activities that are framed around a 'real-life' context in which students become engaged in their learning in my classroom. Authentic learning has become meaningful to each student because it allows the student to draw from his or her own personal life story, and experiences, to make those connections within education."

Students worked in teams of three or four to create solutions to the challenging investigations. Each investigation was assigned four teams to explore potential solutions. During the two-week time period, teams of students met on-site with their business/community partners to immerse themselves in the investigation. Students interviewed experts, conducted research, and brainstormed solutions. Throughout this process, the students continually evaluated their proposals and the basis for their justification. On the Thursday of the second week of the program, the teams of students presented to the experts with whom they had worked. This outside audience determined the winning team for each challenging investigation based on the solution they found to be the most feasible and potentially successful with a possible implementation. The following day, the winning teams from each partnership connection competed in a final round of presentations to a panel of civic leaders, corporate CEOs, and experts, who determined the best overall solution.

Not only did students receive on-site, firsthand career experience, they were also afforded four college credits from Grand Rapids Community College (GRCC), as the two-week experience was aligned to the GRCC Business Innovation course standards. These standards directly line up with the 21st-century skills that organizations such as the Partnership for 21st Century Skills (www.p21.org) advocate. Additionally, they reflect many of the Common Core State Standards.

COMMON CORE STATE STANDARDS

12.RIT.5	Analyze and evaluate the effectiveness of the structure an author uses in his or her exposition or argument, including whether the structure makes points clear, convincing, and engaging.
12.RIT.7	Integrate and evaluate multiple sources of information presented in different media or formats as well as in words in order to address a question or solve a problem.
12.W.1	Write arguments to support claims in an analysis of substantive topics or texts, using valid reasoning and relevant and sufficient evidence.
12.W.2	Write informative/explanatory texts to examine and convey complex ideas, concepts, and information clearly and accurately through the effective selection, organization, and analysis of content.

12.W.4	Produce clear and coherent writing in which the development, organization, and style are appropriate to task, purpose, and audience.
12.W.6	Use technology, including the Internet, to produce, publish, and update individual or shared writing products in response to ongoing feedback, including new arguments or information.
12.W.7	Conduct short as well as more sustained research projects to answer a question or solve a problem; narrow or broaden the inquiry when appropriate; synthesize multiple sources on the subject, demonstrating understanding of the subject under investigation.
12.W.8	Gather relevant information from multiple authoritative print and digital sources, using advanced searches effectively; assess the strengths and limitations of each source in terms of the task, purpose, and audience; integrate information into the text selectively to maintain the flow of ideas, avoiding plagiarism and overreliance on any one source and following a standard format for citation.
12.W.9	Draw evidence from literary or informational texts to support analysis, reflection, and research.
12.W.10	Write routinely over extended time frames and shorter time frames for a range of tasks, purposes, and audiences.
12.SL.1	Initiate and participate effectively in a range of collaborative discussions with diverse partners on grade level topics, texts, and issues, building on others' ideas and expressing their own clearly and persuasively.
12.SL.2	Integrate multiple sources of information presented in diverse formats and media in order to make informed decisions and solve problems, evaluating the credibility and accuracy of each source and noting any discrepancies among data.
12.SL.4	Present information, findings, and supporting evidence, conveying a clear and distinct perspective, such that listeners can follow the line of reasoning, alternative or opposing perspectives are addressed, and the organization, development, substance, and style are appropriate to purpose, audience, and a range of formal and informal tasks.
S.IC.3	Recognize the purposes of and differences among sample surveys, experiments, and observational studies; explain how randomization relates to each.
S.IC.6	Evaluate reports based on data.

Technology Integration

All students relied heavily on the use of iPod touches and iMics as they consolidated and recorded their ideas. Depending on the community partnership, other technology tools varied. Some students used Google SketchUp, and PowerPoint was a staple at the formal presentations.

Teacher Reflection

"Often within the educational community, we stress that students internalize or make learning their own through experiencing or living the content and skills that we want them to have in a real-world context, but this doesn't always happen. Sadly, we also tend to forget about this when working with teachers. 'Confined' to contracted professional development days in which there are no students present, we tend to think about professional development as something that *happens to* teachers as opposed to *an experience we do with* teachers to assist with their personal reflection and growth. While the experiences and skills that the students gained from being immersed in exploring real-world issues in an actual business environment within the IChallengeU program were invaluable, in my opinion the real value of the program rested in the skills and the habits of mind that the participating teachers developed. The teachers themselves were able to practice and refine their skills related to creating authenticity within the IChallengeU program. As a result, when they entered their classrooms again and embarked on implementing an Authentic Learning Experience with their students, they could think to themselves, 'Hey, this isn't so foreign to me. I have already done something like this in the past.'"—Jason Pasatta

CHAPTER 7

— ■ —

Designing Interdisciplinary Authentic Learning Experiences

The real world is not divided into stand-alone subjects, but rather provides an integration of a variety of content. For example, when choosing retirement options, you must apply mathematics to calculate potential returns, understand economics to realize the volatility of the markets, and be able to research the history of the performance of various stock options. Or, at the very least, you must comprehend this array of information as an investment broker presents it to you! The understanding of all of these integrated areas provides the ability to make an informed decision. Students must be granted this experience in the classroom in order to be better prepared for life outside the classroom and to be prepared for the career world. Authentic Learning Experiences create the context in which interdisciplinary curriculum designs make strong connections to prior knowledge and the world in which students live. The experiences also create a connection to community and career contexts.

A Shift in Thinking

Authentic Learning Experiences require a teacher to make a shift in his or her own thinking about how the classroom is structured, content is delivered, and standards are met. Once a teacher becomes comfortable with the design of Authentic Learning Experiences, as described in previous chapters, moving into designing interdisciplinary experiences is recommended, in order to truly reflect the world outside the classroom. As teachers, we must move away from the current educational model, which is based on separate subjects with separate textbooks and strictly scheduled time slots for classes and specials. While it may be difficult for schools that are married to a strict bell agenda to do away with scheduled times for individual classes, it is possible to overcome the separate-subjects and separate-textbook mentality. If we truly want to bring authenticity into the classroom, this shift in thinking is necessary. Working deeply in a particular content area that promotes critical thinking is valuable, but realizing that every profession in the world requires integrated perspectives and the intertwining of knowledge from a variety of disciplines will propel teachers to the next level of authenticity. Thus, creating interdisciplinary Authentic Learning Experiences directly guides students to make connections between the classroom and the world in which they live. Figure 7.1 (below) summarizes the things to avoid when creating interdisciplinary connections.

Figure 7.1   Don't Do This . . . When Creating Interdisciplinary Connections

Don't . . .

- Force an interdisciplinary connection when there isn't one. You and your students will become frustrated!
- Design an interdisciplinary experience for you and several teachers without input from the teachers. They will likely bail out of the experience or not put as much effort into it as you and your students, as they don't have any investment in the experience.
- Expect it to go smoothly the first time you implement it.

So what does an interdisciplinary approach to Authentic Learning Experiences look like? If we truly want to create an educational atmosphere where students are engaging in the problem-solving experiences that mirror the daily work lives of professionals, there are two possible approaches. Either a single teacher creates an Authentic Learning Experience that integrates multiple disciplines into one experience, or the experience is carried over several content areas and involves multiple teachers and multiple classes.

The Single-Teacher Approach

In this case, a teacher works alone in creating the experience and only one set of students is focused on completing that experience. This is similar to a professional who works in semi-isolation but integrates the knowledge of many different content areas to complete his or her work. For example, an independent clinical psychiatrist needs to know his or her specialized area of psychiatry, law, pharmacology, and accounting, not to mention he or she must be an M.D. before even starting a psychiatric residency!

The single-teacher approach is a great place for teachers to start in the process of creating interdisciplinary experiences. For example, in a history class that is studying wars and conflicts, the teacher could bring in elements of math through the analysis of death tolls in each war of the 20th century. English language arts could be addressed as students read selected fiction and nonfiction works related to various 20th-century wars in a literature circle–type fashion. Additionally, science could be added to the Authentic Learning Experience through the study of the effects of chemical warfare starting in World War I and how it related to the changing tactical methods for fighting. All these elements could be combined to focus on the final product of an Authentic Learning Experience centered on creating a plan for the removal of U.S. troops from foreign deployments based on lessons learned from historical wars. This plan could then be presented to a group of veterans. Or, as mentioned in Chapter 1, the plan could be proposed to a soldier currently serving on foreign soil. The presentation could take place either in person or through Web capabilities such as Skype or via a presentation created with a Web 2.0 tool like Prezi, which could be shared with the veterans or serving soldier. An additional example of this single-teacher approach in practice is the Authentic Learning Experience in an elementary school described later in this chapter.

The single-teacher approach does not require a lot of logistical finagling on your part. You have your students and know your content and standards. You don't have to worry about scheduling conflicts related to the time at which you teach a particular unit versus another teacher's time frame, assuming you even have the same set of students. Additionally, you won't have to worry about managing to get groups of students together for an experience if they do not meet at the same time. Not to mention, the effort it might take to connect different sets of students in different schools doesn't have to be considered! However, once you have mastered the design of an Authentic Learning Experience in your content area alone, but before you embark on a planning frenzy with your colleagues in other content areas, it is advisable to give the single-teacher approach a shot. This is a great time to try incorporating the math and English language arts/literacy Common Core State Standards that were discussed in Chapter 6.

> ## ☑ Check for Understanding
>
> Choose your next unit of study. Align any other content areas that you think will fit with your curriculum. Ask your colleagues with the appropriate expertise to review your notes to determine the viability of your choices.

The Multiple-Teacher Approach

In the multiple-teacher approach, teachers work together across content areas to create an Authentic Learning Experience. While this requires a great deal of planning, collaboration, and scheduling on the part of all teachers involved, the payoff is well worth the effort. This scenario does not necessarily mean that all teachers involved need to have the same students. In fact, it is completely possible that multiple sets of students from different classes with different teachers are working toward the same end goal, each with a different focus. For example, an art teacher could partner with a government teacher in a collaborative effort of "Art Meets Politics." The goal of the art students would be to create sculptures showcasing political perspectives of current public policy to showcase in the state's capitol building. The goal of the government students would be to write proposed legislation related to the public policy to present to a legislative representative. In this example, the art students have the technical background for creating sculptures, while the government students have the political knowledge on public policy. The two groups would work in conjunction to support one another with their content area expertise.

While this multiple-teacher approach works well with different students, there is a convenience to having the same students, with different teachers taking on different responsibilities within the Authentic Learning Experience. Having the same students also promotes a greater connection between the content areas for the students involved. An example is a program that revolves around one theme, such as conflict resolution. Perhaps the sociology class would investigate an issue such as domestic violence and propose ways to address it. These solutions would be shared with a panel of experts that might include personnel from the local victims' rights group, a family court judge, and a local state representative. The media literacy class could use the research conducted by the sociology class to create public service announcements to play on the high school television station about the same topic as a means of informing the student body. The PSA could also be distributed to the local news station for possible airing or, at the very least, for professional feedback. Nonetheless, the reality for most teaching situations is that common students across disciplines is a rarity unless you are teaching on a middle school team, in a pure career academy model school, or in a small magnet or charter school. However, this obstacle can be overcome.

> ☑ **Check for Understanding**
> Find two or three colleagues with whom you'd like to partner for your next Authentic Learning Experience. Spend a planning period, in-service afternoon, or lunch break mapping out the content that each of you teaches. Find the commonalities and connections between your content areas. Determine the strongest connections and begin to sketch out your interdisciplinary Authentic Learning Experience.
> Note: If time is not available during the school day, the planning session can take place online via a collaborative tool such as Google Drive.

In planning for a multiple-teacher approach to an Authentic Learning Experience, teachers should start with a common goal. This goal should be broad enough to draw on multiple disciplines. Beginning with one other teacher is advisable for those who are starting out. However, I have witnessed entire middle school teams of teachers working in concert with one another as well as with the "specials" (i.e., art, music, and physical education) teachers to create one Authentic Learning Experience. In either case, the outcome is an amazing one for students in terms of learning and authentic connections. The high school example provided in this chapter is a perfect illustration of how the multiple-teacher approach created a successful interdisciplinary Authentic Learning Experience. The middle school example also uses the multiple-teacher approach. While only two teachers and two subjects were used, there are also elements of the single-teacher approach in this multidisciplinary experience.

Interdisciplinary Examples

Farms and Food: Providing Healthy Food to All People

Nicole Weiner and Heidi Fessenden
Young Achievers Science and Mathematics Pilot School
Boston, Massachusetts

School Background

This is an urban pilot school that is a part of the Boston Public Schools. The school's focus is on math and science. However, art, music, technology, and physical education are embedded in the curriculum. Special education is an inclusive program, and paraprofessionals are assigned to each classroom. Class sizes are limited to eighteen students.

Challenging Investigation

Where does our food come from, and how does it feed our community?

Authentic Learning Experience Description

First-grade students spent a year immersed in the study of farms and foods. The details provided cover the following content areas:

- art
- math
- reading
- social studies
- health
- nutrition
- science
- writing

Students engaged in soil studies, worked on-site at various local farms, read fiction and nonfiction works on nutrition and foods, and even studied Cesar Chavez and the movement to improve social justice for farm workers.

Students began their Authentic Learning Experience with a trip to a local apple orchard, but they focused the majority of their studies at a local farm, thus beginning their first community connection. Study groups formed around the topics of bees, fruits, vegetables and grains, and poultry. These study groups worked with field experts and conducted hands-on work both on-site and in the classroom. Hands-on activities included farm work, incubation of chicks, cooking, sketching, taste testing, retelling, sequencing, sorting, and data collection. The study groups were responsible for creating a chapter for the class *Farm Book* in which the justification element was met through a validation of the inclusion of their entries to their classmates. Each student read excerpts from this book to an outside audience of parents at an exhibition night.

Throughout the year, as a result of their in-depth study of the challenging investigation, students planted, maintained, and harvested a class garden. The science behind the growth of plants was the focus during this phase of the Authentic Learning Experience. A measurement of the growth of plants was also an integral part of the Authentic Learning Experience.

Finally, students investigated the social justice issue of homelessness and used their harvested food to help to provide portions of meals to a local homeless shelter, as the second component of their community connection. In conjunction with this segment of the project, students created a full-color calendar containing student writing and art.

The calendar incorporated ideas on how healthy food could be made accessible to all people and ways that individuals could help the environment through recycling efforts. Again, the justification element was met in this portion of the Authentic Learning Experience, as students had to defend their reasons before selecting items for inclusion. They then donated the proceeds from the calendar sales to the organizations that helped the students during the Authentic Learning Experience. These community organizations included the local homeless shelter, the local food bank, the community gardens, and a local soup kitchen.

COMMON CORE STATE STANDARDS

1.RL.3	Describe characters, settings, and major events in a story, using key details.
1.RL.5	Explain major differences between books that tell stories and books that give information, drawing on a wide reading of a range of text types.
1.RIT.8	Identify the reasons an author gives to support points in a text.
1.W.2	Write informative/explanatory texts in which they name a topic, supply some facts about the topic, and provide some sense of closure.
1.W.5	With guidance and support from adults, focus on a topic, respond to questions and suggestions from peers, and add details to strengthen writing as needed.
1.SL.1	Participate in collaborative conversations with diverse partners about grade 1 topics and texts with peer and adults in small and larger groups.

1.SL.5	Add drawings or other visual displays to descriptions when appropriate to clarify ideas, thoughts, and feelings.
1.OA.5	Relate counting to addition and subtraction (e.g., by counting on 2 to add 2).
1.MD.1	Order three objects by length; compare the lengths of two objects indirectly by using a third object.
1.MD.4	Organize, represent, and interpret data with up to three categories.

Technology Integration

When students were ready to prepare their final drafts, the project was moved to the computer lab. Students were initially taught how to log in to the computers, and each student received his or her own login. This was the first time students received instruction on word processing. While the technology used was basic, it is one of the most important and useful technology skills students need to master! Teacher Heidi Fessenden explained how using simple keys such as the space bar is such an achievement for first-grade students, as one push of the space bar never seems to be enough for them. Students also learned the importance of the Shift key and how to undo their typing. After a week of word processing, peer editing, and teacher editing, the final products were ready for publication.

Teacher Reflection

"In first grade, the Farms and Food unit infuses much of what we do every day. Because we are thinking about it in math, during read-alouds, during writing, and in our Experiential Ed block at the end of the day, it becomes a living, breathing thing instead of just a 'unit.' It also makes the isolated skills that need to be taught in first grade much more meaningful. Students learn, for example, to capitalize the first word of the sentence as they type their final draft of their Farm Book page or how to make a graph to show the results of a taste test between store-bought and farm-fresh eggs. Not only do these academic skills seem important because of the context of the final projects, but students gain a deeper understanding of communities: those near our school and in our city as well as those outside of the city that they would otherwise not have access to. Many of our students don't really understand that milk comes from a cow, for example; so visiting the farm makes a huge impression. They start to talk, during lunchtime, about where each food on their tray came from. They learn how to plant seeds and watch those seeds turn into plants, which we then eat. They see ways that activists in the city are dedicating their lives to making sure everyone has access to healthy food. It all comes together over the course of the year in such a meaningful way, and they are *so proud* of their work when it comes time for the family presentation—which is, in the end, another way to connect back to the most important members of their communities—their families."—Heidi Fessenden

Cubs That Care!

Mary Durand and Jeremy Weilert
Humboldt Middle School
Humboldt, Kansas

School Background

Humboldt Middle School services students in a rural, agricultural area in southeastern Kansas. The small school has approximately 150 students, with nearly half of its population on free or reduced-cost lunch plans. The school is deeply committed to technology integration and providing students with opportunities to "develop a sense of citizenship, respect for self, others, and the environment."

Challenging Investigation

How can we make crosswalks, sidewalks, and road conditions safer for our community of walkers and bicyclers?

Authentic Learning Experience Description

In a quest to get students actively involved in the learning process, after receiving a Kansas Technology Rich Classroom Grant, students in Mary Durand's seventh-grade Extended Learning Period class were asked a question: "What in your community do you feel needs improving?" Students quickly started brainstorming ideas and then grouped themselves according to similar interests to take on a community action plan and began to investigate potential areas of concern. After creating and presenting persuasive PowerPoint presentations embedded with video and pictures to the student body for voting, the class decided on reducing the potential for accidents in their community for those who walked or rode bicycles to school. The seventh-grade math students, with some data-gathering help from Jeremy Weilert's sixth-grade social studies class, applied their mathematical skills as they collected data and distributed surveys. Students also took photographs, and videotaped traffic areas of concern as they began answering the challenging investigation. As the experience progressed, students were faced with a few real-life challenges that were unanticipated! Construction closed down a section of road that the students were initially focused on improving. In fact, traffic was rerouted, making the original area of concern a moot issue. Thus, the students decided to shift their focus to the area directly in front of their school. Additionally, bad weather conditions during the initial stages of the experience postponed a bit of their data collection. As the students, in due time, gathered and analyzed the data, they were able to provide a detailed justification process in a formal presentation to an outside audience, the school administration and school board. Students were immediately able to see the results of their work, as school crossing guards were put in place after their convincing arguments were presented to the administrative team.

The following school year, the experience continued as the now eighth-grade math students shifted their focus to a grant opportunity through the Safe Routes to School program. Students again gathered data and completed an analysis of that data to create an action plan, which was presented at another forum for an outside audience connection. At a community town hall meeting, students presented their data to once again promote the justification of their proposed plan. In order to make the students' vision for improvements possible, the community support from the town hall meeting led to a formal grant proposal to the Kansas Department of Transportation. The students asked for $250,000 to make improvements to the sidewalks around the school. These enhancements included better signage for motorists and pedestrians, curb improvements to be in compliance with the Americans with Disabilities Act, sidewalk renovations, and the realignment of crosswalks. The students were finalists in the grant selection process and had to walk the selection committee around to show them the improvements they intended make. Unfortunately, the students were not the grant award recipients, but this in and of itself was a learning lesson for the students.

COMMON CORE STATE STANDARDS

7.W.1	Write arguments to support claims with clear reasons and relevant evidence.
7.W.2	Write informative/explanatory texts to examine a topic and convey ideas, concepts, and information through the selection, organization, and analysis of relevant content.
7.W.7	Conduct short research projects to answer a question, drawing on several sources and generating additional related, focused questions for further research and investigation.
7.SL.4	Present claims and findings, emphasizing salient points in a focused, coherent manner with pertinent descriptions, facts, details, and examples; use appropriate eye contact, adequate volume, and clear pronunciation.

7.SL.5	Include multimedia components and visual displays in presentations to clarify claims and findings and emphasize salient points.
7.NS.3	Solve real-world and mathematical problems involving the four operations with rational numbers.
7.SP.1	Understand that statistics can be used to gain information about a population by examining a sample of the population; generalizations about a population from a sample are valid only if the sample is representative of that population. Understand that random sampling tends to produce representative samples and support valid inferences.
7.SP.5	Understand that the probability of a chance event is a number between 0 and 1 that expresses the likelihood of the event occurring. Larger numbers indicate greater likelihood. A probability near 0 indicates an unlikely event, a probability around ½ indicates an event that is neither unlikely nor likely, and a probability near 1 indicates a likely event.
7.SP.7	Develop a probability model and use it to find probabilities of events. Compare probabilities from a model to observed frequencies; if the agreement is not good, explain possible sources of the discrepancy.
8.F.4	Construct a function to model a linear relationship between two quantities. Determine the rate of change and initial value of the function from a description of a relationship or from two (x, y) values, including reading these from a table or from a graph. Interpret the rate of change and initial value of a linear function in terms of the situation it models, and in terms of its graph or a table of values.
8.F.5	Describe qualitatively the functional relationship between two quantities by analyzing a graph (e.g., where the function is increasing or decreasing, linear or nonlinear). Sketch a graph that exhibits the qualitative features of a function that has been described verbally.
8.SP.1	Construct and interpret scatter plots for bivariate measurement data to investigate patterns of association between two quantities. Describe patterns such as clustering, outliers, positive or negative association, linear association, and nonlinear association.
8.SP.3	Use the equation of a linear model to solve problems in the context of bivariate measurement data, interpreting the slope and intercept.
8.SP.4	Understand that patterns of association can also be seen in bivariate categorical data by displaying frequencies and relative frequencies in a two-way table. Construct and interpret a two-way table summarizing data on two categorical variables collected from the same subjects. Use relative frequencies calculated for rows or columns to describe possible association between the two variables.

Technology Integration

Students used Flip cameras to take the video necessary for analysis and to help in the justification of the need for improvements to the targeted areas. This video was also incorporated into a Movie Maker presentation. Students graphed their findings in Excel and used both PowerPoint and Word to complete their presentations, create the surveys, and write the proposals.

Teacher Reflection

"I feel the most important part of the Cubs That Care! experience was the voice it gave to my students despite their age. They worked as professionals collecting, analyzing, and presenting data in such a manner that raised awareness in their community. They enhanced their communication skills, as they had to communicate through discussions, presentations, and written materials— presenting their concerns in a variety of formats. They conducted presentations to their peers, the administration, the school board, the city council, and community members through a town hall meeting, and finally to the grant review committee in the final stages of the grant selection process. Unfortunately, they also had to accept the reality of not being chosen as this year's recipient of the grant. I believe this experience has made each student involved a better citizen of their community and will help them create a voice for themselves in the future by providing them the knowledge and skills to be an effective communicator and instigator of change."
—Mary Durand

Foundations:
The Learning Landscape

Eric White, Lindsey Ott, and Ben Williams
The G School/Coahulla Creek High School
Dalton, Georgia

School Description

The G School is a "school within a school" in Coahulla Creek High School. Student numbers are limited to sixty, and the G School model seeks to empower these students to "think differently, take risks, innovate, and collaborate on real and relevant challenges."

Challenging Investigation

How can we redesign classroom furniture to be more suitable for a 21st-century learning environment?

Authentic Learning Experience Description

The G School was approached by a fifth-grade class at the local elementary school that was in need of a First Lego League table for their international robotics competitions. The challenging investigation organically grew out of the subsequent conversations the G School students had with the elementary class of students and their teacher. Students formed design teams and crafted interview questions to elicit the needs of the classroom, which, it turned out, went far beyond a First Lego League table. It was determined that the learning space, as it was designed, did not facilitate the collaborative approach that 21st-century learning targets. Nor did the classroom contain any of the personal touches the G School students felt were important for the elementary students to experience.

In the initial stages of the student work, ten design specifications were distributed based on functionality, mobility, storage, size, aesthetics, learnability, sustainability, durability, feasibility, and stability. Student design teams were able to choose four areas on which to focus their efforts and also chose a particular piece of furniture to redesign. These design specifications were later used in conjunction with the justification element of the Authentic Learning

Experience, as all furniture had to meet the given requirements. To get the students thinking about the engineering process, a spaghetti bridge-building activity was incorporated as part of the scaffolding process for the larger context of the challenging investigation. In this activity, students had to test load capacities on bridges constructed of no more than twenty spaghetti noodles. In this portion of the process, students began to master some of the much-needed scientific core concepts and engineering principles.

As the Authentic Learning Experience evolved over a series of weeks, the students were not only exposed to the engineering and math of designing the furniture, but they also integrated fine arts through the graphic design process. Additionally, the core components of social studies classrooms were stressed, with a clear focus on the anthropology connections dealing with human interaction in an environment. Students also incorporated the ELA components of conducting research and writing to support their findings, which would ultimately be presented to their outside audience, the fifth-grade class for whom they were "working."

The furniture designs underwent a series of refinements as students prototyped their work. The first low-resolution prototypes were done on graph paper and then built using cardboard. Students once again worked through the justification process as they determined whether their designs were feasible. The outside audience, the fifth-grade class, also reviewed the prototypes and provided feedback that was taken into consideration in the high-level prototype refinement. This series of prototypes included a large-scale drawing, a 3-D model, and a digital representation created using Google SketchUp. After further feedback and revision, the furniture designs were ready for production.

In the final stages of this Authentic Learning Experience, students participated in a safety seminar and had to pass a safety examination before commencing the final building process. As the fifth-grade students were actually going to use this furniture, precision and care were of the utmost importance to the G School students. Once the pieces were complete, the presentation of the furniture was a celebration of learning and connecting with the greater school community. After school hours, the G School students installed the furniture, which included a First Lego League table, storage units, a learning loft, a mobile teacher workstation, and hexagon-shaped student desks. The next day the G School students presented their work to their enthusiastic outside audience. During this presentation, the students shared their design process and provided the justification for their design plans. One fifth-grade student said, "I love that everything is movable and on wheels. You guys rock!"

COMMON CORE STATE STANDARDS

11. RIT.7	Integrate and evaluate multiple sources of information presented in different media or formats (e.g., visually, quantitatively) as well as in words in order to address a question or solve a problem.
11.W.1	Write arguments to support claims in an analysis of substantive topics or texts, using valid reasoning and relevant and sufficient evidence.
11.W.2	Write informative/explanatory texts to examine and convey complex ideas, concepts, and information clearly and accurately through the effective selection, organization, and analysis of content.
11.W.4	Produce clear and coherent writing in which the development, organization, and style are appropriate to task, purpose, and audience.
11.W.5	Develop and strengthen writing as needed by planning, revising, editing, rewriting, or trying a new approach, focusing on addressing what is most significant for a specific purpose and audience.
11.W.7	Conduct short as well as more sustained research projects to answer a question (including a self-generated question) to solve a problem; narrow or broaden the inquiry when appropriate; synthesize multiple sources on the subject, demonstrating understanding of the subject under investigation.
11.SL.1	Initiate and participate effectively in a range of collaborative discussions (one-on-one, in groups, and teacher-led) with diverse partners on grades 11–12 topics, texts, and issues, building on others' ideas and expressing their own clearly and persuasively.
11.SL.4	Present information, findings, and supporting evidence, conveying a clear and distinct perspective, such that listeners can follow the line of reasoning, alternative or opposing perspectives are addressed, and the organization, development, substance, and style are appropriate to purpose, audience, and a range of formal and informal tasks.
G.CO.5	Given a geometric figure and a rotation, reflection, or translation, draw the transformed figure using, e.g., graph paper, tracing paper, or geometry software. Specify a sequence of transformations that will carry a given figure onto another.
G.CO.12	Make formal geometric constructions with a variety of tools and methods.
G.MG.1	Use geometric shapes, their measures, and their properties to describe objects.
G.MG.3	Apply geometric methods to solve design problems (e.g., designing an object or structure to satisfy physical constraints or minimize cost; working with typographic grid systems based on ratios).

| **G.GMD.4** | Identify the shapes of two-dimensional cross-sections of three-dimensional objects, and identify three-dimensional objects generated by rotations of two-dimensional objects. |

Technology Integration

After the G School students videotaped their interviews with the fifth-grade class, they produced movies of the interviews utilizing iMovie and Movie Maker. Google SketchUp was also used to aid in the construction of the 3-D renderings of their furniture designs.

Teacher Reflection

"Throughout the duration of this project, I noticed tremendous growth in my students, particularly in the areas of collaboration, creative confidence, critical thinking, and problem solving. Many of them took such ownership of their designs that they 'stepped out of the shadows' in order to be heard. As I look back at the design challenge as a whole, I think we missed a few opportunities to capitalize on that ownership and drive home some sophisticated engineering concepts to the group. For example, small groups learned a variety of concepts such as rotational mass, torsional flex, and torsional rigidity, among others. We could have taken those principles and exploded the lesson to reach all of the groups working on various designs. It is really critical that we stay on the lookout for those 'teachable moments' for the group. I really couldn't believe the sophisticated designs the students created and the 'meaty' concepts we had to use to bring them to life!"
—Lindsey Ott

CHAPTER 8

— ■ —

Authentic Assessment

My beliefs about assessment can be quickly summarized into two points:

- Formative assessments are a much better representation of student growth and learning than summative assessments.
- End-of-the-unit tests are not an accurate picture of student learning.

I realize that many of you won't be immediately ready to take the leap to eliminate unit tests. However, after implementing Authentic Learning Experiences in your own classroom, you may just change your mind. I did, after eleven years of teaching! At the very least, you probably have your feet wet when it comes to formative assessment and can use that familiarity to help you further develop your implementation of Authentic Learning Experiences.

Formative Assessment: What Is It, Anyway?

A few years ago, while sitting in a department curriculum meeting listening to a discussion on formative and summative assessment, I realized how clueless I was about the topic. I had no idea how to define either and made it a point to Google the terms as soon as I wasn't under the watchful eyes of my colleagues! Once I discovered the definitions, I quickly ascertained that I did very little formative assessment or ongoing assessment throughout the learning process. My idea of assessing students was limited to a reading quiz (if I remembered to create one) and an end-of-the-unit test that required students to do a lot of memorization, a little bit of application, and maybe a document analysis. My assessments were certainly more summative in nature, as I waited until the end to determine students' understanding of the content and concepts. My students were all over the board in terms of grades. I'm not even sure I had a bell curve! The good test takers did well, and the others did not. I would provide students with the opportunity to make test corrections to earn back half the points they had missed. This, I thought, was a best practice. Students would look up the correct answers and provide explanations for them. They would "learn" without the need to take additional precious class time to reteach the concepts, vocabulary, and standards. Boy, was I off track! Don't get me wrong; I still give my AP students an end-of-the-unit test. I almost consider it a necessary evil. They have to "learn" how to take a multiple-choice test for the AP Exam in May. I also still allow those students the opportunity to make test corrections. However, in all other courses that I teach, I have eliminated my end-of-the-unit tests over the last four years and have used the cumulative end products in my Authentic Learning Experiences to summatively assess my students' learning.

Shifting to a more methodical manner of formatively assessing students, rather than relying on mere teacher observation, has become a necessary practice to ensure the success of my Authentic Learning Experiences. I've had to deliberately incorporate a variety of methods to continually assess the progression of my students' skill development, understanding of the key concepts, and ability to think critically. While it takes both time and a conscious effort on my part, the end results of my students' learning have been significantly improved.

Effective Formative Assessment

Figure 8.1 (page 139) summarizes important tools for formative assessment. One of these tools is journal writing. Daily journal reflections are one of the best predictors of how well your students understand the challenging investigation. Whether online or in the traditional paper format, a blog or journal entry at the end of the class period causes a student to pause and think about the research, data analysis, expert opinion consultations, and collaborative efforts that have occurred. There is a need for students to deliberately process this information. Often students gather information but don't consider what implications that information has on their ability to answer the challenging investigation. Thus, writing a simple paragraph or two is a great way for students to stop and reflect on their understanding

Figure 8.1 Formative Assessment Tools

- Daily journal entries
- Spiderweb discussion
- Fishbowl discussion
- Socratic seminar
- Recorded discussions (audio or online)
- Individual meetings
- Team meetings

and a powerful way in which you can begin to determine student growth and understanding. These journal entries help you to craft any scaffolding lessons and to differentiate for students. They also map a progression of the understanding that students gain during the course of the experience and are evidence that can be shared with students, parents, or case managers when determining learning goals and targets for students. The rubric in Figure 8.2 (below) can help you target your assessment of student journals.

Figure 8.2 Journal Entry Rubric

	2	3	4	5
Entries Completed	Completed less than 50 percent of the entries	Completed between 50 percent and 75 percent of the entries	Completed more than 75 percent, but fewer than 90 percent of the entries	Completed 90 percent or more of the entries
Quality of Entries	Entries were less than satisfactory.	Entries were of satisfactory quality.	Entries were of good quality.	Entries were of excellent quality.
Relation to Challenging Investigation	Entries did not relate to the challenging investigation.	Entries touched upon the challenging investigation.	Entries predominantly related to the challenging investigation.	Entries related solely to the challenging investigation.
Reflection	Entries were not reflective.	Entries were occasionally reflective.	Entries were usually reflective.	Entries were always reflective.
Spelling and Grammar	There were ten or more grammar or spelling errors.	There were five or more grammar or spelling errors.	There were fewer than five grammar or spelling errors.	There were no grammar or spelling errors.
			Total Points Earned: _____ /25	

Discussion tools are paramount for students to verbalize their learning. While there are many ways that discussion-type formative assessments can be implemented, it is important to remember that merely hovering over a group conversation doesn't give teachers enough information to fully process and determine the understanding and subsequent needs of students. Certainly, informal scans of group conversations can be telling in their own right, but gleaned information isn't detailed enough to do substantial formative assessment. Use the scans to determine when it may be appropriate to implement one of the discussion-type assessments.

The use of spiderweb discussions is one of my favorite tools. It is largely based on the Harkness discussion method developed by Phillips Exeter Academy that was introduced to me by Kelly O'Connor. Let students sit in a circle, and plot the names of the students on a circular chart. Give the students a critical-thinking prompt, and then sit back and simply chart the progress of the students. Draw a line to connect the names each time a new student speaks to another student. The goal, at the end of the discussion, is to have a well-balanced spiderweb effect on your chart. If the chart looks like that well-balanced spiderweb, all students pass the discussion. If not, the group does not pass. A student who brings the discussion back on point, engages another student who isn't participating, or adds significant depth to the conversation can earn extra points. While this may seem a bit harsh, keep in mind the points earned are relatively minimal in the scheme of things. I typically keep it to fifteen points per discussion. Additionally, the first several times I conduct this type of a discussion, I allow students who don't participate to earn the points back by writing a short reflection of what they would have said in the conversation. By the third time implementing this method, students self-monitor, can predict the spiderweb design, and usually agree who should receive the additional points. It is an excellent way to monitor group understanding and individual misconceptions and can be done in a large group of up to thirty students or in much smaller groups of ten to twelve, as the original Harkness method intended.

The use of a modified fishbowl discussion is another way to keep students on their toes in relation to formative assessment. While you can certainly implement a traditional fishbowl, I prefer a modified version that allows for more participation. I utilize five chairs at the front of the room and do not leave an empty chair. Students in the fishbowl are prompted to discuss a topic related to the challenging investigation. Any student who is not in the fishbowl can tag into the discussion at any time if he or she wants to comment. The students who are not in the fishbowl can "back channel" during the discussion via an online tool such as TitanPad. If online tools are not available, more traditional paper-and-pencil individual reflections can take place during the discussion.

> ### ✔ Check for Understanding
> Choose one of the formative assessment practices listed in this section, and implement the exercise during your next department or faculty meeting. Debrief the experience and determine points to ponder and ways to implement the practice in your own classroom.

Socratic seminars should not be reserved for older students. Even our youngest students are able to delve deeply into the inquiry process, as has been evidenced in the elementary Authentic Learning Experience examples provided in the previous chapters. However, at any grade level, the modeling process is yet again an extremely important part of successful implementation. In the Socratic seminar, students are prompted to ask one another open-ended questions rather than simply comment on or debate about a topic. With younger students, the teacher may have to create the bulk of the questions to guide the process. It is conceivable that this may need to occur at the upper-level grades as well until the procedure is well established and practiced a number of times. I often like to run simultaneous small-group Socratic seminars to ensure a greater deal of participation and overall comfort with the process. This also allows students to rotate through the responsibility of being in the "hot seat," as I like to call it. Thus, it may be necessary to videotape the seminars in order to actively assess each student's critical-thinking capabilities. Students can reflect on the seminar and critique one another on the understanding of the information. It is also helpful in creating next steps for promoting critical thinking about the challenging investigation.

In the past, I have used small-group discussions that were recorded via GarageBand or another recording device. Student groups were prompted with a critical-thinking question related to the content being applied to the challenging investigation. This was effective for the students, but it took me twenty minutes or more to listen to each of the conversations, and I had to be able to discern the different voices! I switched to online discussions via TitanPad and was able to simultaneously monitor six or seven group conversations at once. I was also able to participate in each of the conversations as I tabbed through each of the online discussions open in my Web browser. If an online tool or recording device is not available, it is possible to schedule small-group discussions to take place one at a time while you simply monitor and take notes. This method certainly involves more logistical planning, but it can be accomplished; one group could meet while the other groups are engaged in another segment of the challenging investigation, for example.

Use the rubric in Figure 8.3 (below), or modify it for your own needs, when scoring online discussions between students.

Figure 8.3   Online Discussion Rubric

	1	2	3	4
Level of Participation	Participated very little.	Participated, but not frequently.	Frequent participation.	Participation was above and beyond what was expected.
Discussion Points	Discussion conducted did not add to thread.	Discussion was basic with some points to add.	Discussion was thoughtful.	Discussion was insightful.
Appropriateness of Discussion	Discussion was oftentimes inappropriate.	Discussion was sometimes inappropriate.	Discussion had one inappropriate section.	Discussion was always appropriate.
Conventions	Improper conventions used frequently.	Improper conventions used infrequently.	Proper conventions were attempted.	Proper conventions were followed.
			Total Points Earned ____ X 2 = ____	

All the aforementioned types of formative assessments will take time to implement effectively. Not only do you have to schedule the time in which to conduct the discussions, but you also have to model the process for the students. We can't expect students to jump into the discussions on the first try with a high level of success. Many students aren't used to participating orally in class, and this can be an uncomfortable situation. You have to create a culture of acceptance of ideas and demand a level of respect for a variety of ideas and beliefs. You will also, more than likely, have to use a point system to assess students. Over time, you may be able to diminish this practice, but

I have found that using a simple rubric based on participation, evidence of critical thinking, and openness to the ideas of others gives me the ability to chart progress. Unfortunately, students, parents, and administrators are typically attuned to and attached to grades. Assigning points for these formative assessment practices gives you the ability to address any concerns that these parties may have, as well as gives you a benchmark indicator of what supports you may need to put in place for each of your students.

Individual and group meetings are an important part of assessing not only content knowledge and critical thinking about the content, but also collaboration among students if they are working in teams. Try to schedule at least two group meetings and two individual meetings per Authentic Learning Experience. It is important to conduct both types of meetings, as you will surely receive two different perspectives. The group mentality may be very different from the mind-set of a student speaking with you one-on-one. Keep the meetings short and on schedule. Have students sign up for five-minute meetings and delve into any issues that you have already determined based on other formative assessments you have been conducting. These meetings can be scheduled during class time; there is not a need to provide before-school and after-school meeting hours unless you are compelled to do so.

I use the rubric in Figure 8.4 (page 144) that I created in conjunction with my colleague Erin Walker for both individual and group meetings. The goal of the meetings, whether individual or group, is the same. Students should take the initiative to schedule the meetings and to show up for the meetings. Additionally, students should be prepared to discuss their progress on the challenging investigation with you.

Whatever formative assessment practices you employ during the course of an Authentic Learning Experience, be sure to utilize the information to further guide your implementation process. Formative assessment will help you to monitor the growth of each student and make determinations for supporting each student to better instruct your decisions on how to differentiate as needed. Thus, Authentic Learning Experiences, while created for a class as a whole, can and should be tailored to each student.

Summative Assessment Is More Than Just a Test

Standardized tests are a part of education today. Unfortunately, it is unlikely that they are going to go away. However, the way in which students are uniformly tested is evolving. Think back to the examples provided in Chapter 6 on the Common Core related to the PARCC and SBAC tests.

Figure 8.4   Progress Meeting Rubric

	1	2	3	4
Scheduled Meeting	Student did not take the initiative to schedule a progress meeting.	Student scheduled progress meeting but did not show up.	Student scheduled and showed up for the progress meeting and was mostly prepared for the discussion.	Student scheduled and showed up for the progress meeting and was entirely prepared for the discussion.
Demonstration of Critical Thinking	Student was unable to answer questions posed.	Student was able to answer all questions posed but demonstrated very little critical thinking.	Student was able to answer most questions posed and demonstrated critical thinking about those concepts.	Student was able to openly discuss topics and demonstrated critical thinking related to the ongoing investigation.
On-Task Behavior Determinations	Student did not demonstrate staying on task based on a lack of materials completed at the progress meeting.	Student is clearly on task based on presented materials completed at the progress meeting.	N/A	N/A

Total Points Earned (first meeting): _____/10

Total Points Earned (second meeting): _____/10

OVERALL POINTS EARNED: _____/20

Questions from those tests require students to think critically rather than simply memorize content. The College Board is also in the process of revamping its Advanced Placement tests and courses. AP Biology is one of the first courses to have its exam undergo a series of reformations. Several additional courses and exams are slated for renewal in the upcoming school years. While the tests are still partially focused on multiple-choice questions, these questions have changed from content-specific to application questions. Thus, it can be inferred that many standardized tests will follow suit in the near future. However, it is still perfectly acceptable to provide your students with opportunities to engage in test preparation. I generally spend a day each unit practicing AP Exam questions with my government students. There are certainly helpful hints you can provide on the ways in which questions are written, and practicing the written responses to the essay questions is beneficial to students.

Please continue to test your students if you find it necessary or if your district requires it as a component of unit grades. However, changing the way in which you test your students to reflect a focus on critical thinking and application of the content studied during the Authentic Learning Experience is important. I would encourage you to place more of an emphasis on the end product of the Authentic Learning Experience rather than the test. You will probably find that many students are better able to exhibit an understanding of the content through a presentation, a letter, or a final exhibit. You will also need to incorporate a written component in which students reflect on their learning. For example, the presentation that my students did on ways to end the troop occupation in Afghanistan, which was a team effort, also included an individual component in which each student wrote a reflective essay. The essay required a minimum of two examples from each of the 20th-century wars to support the final proposal on how to successfully remove the U.S. troops. Thus, I was not only able to assess collaboration and critical thinking, but I was also able to assess students' communication skills.

> ### ☑ Check for Understanding
> Work with a teaching partner to revamp a current end-of-the-unit test. Practice rewriting the questions to focus on critical-thinking skills in which students are required to apply the knowledge and skills gained, rather than the information memorized. Share your work for review at an upcoming department meeting.

Final components for inclusion on a summative assessment can take many forms, depending on the goals for your Authentic Learning Experience. I would, however, encourage you to include many of the components I've listed in Figure 8.5 (page 146). It is also advisable to create rubrics that are similar in nature no matter what the end product is for the challenging investigation. Therefore, your levels of competency for any of the components would look the same for every investigation. I use this method of rubric implementation to ensure students know what to expect when they are assessed. I also use this method to tailor my assessments to each student.

Creating very broad categories permits me to differentiate as needed. Using the same rubric, my assessment of a high-level Gifted-IEP student can be completed just as my assessment of a very low-level IEP student can.

Figure 8.5   Summative Assessment Rubric Elements

- Research
- Critical thinking
- Justification process
- Creativity
- Knowledge gained
- Professionalism
- Collaboration

My students complete individual reflection assessments of their work at the completion of the Authentic Learning Experience that I include in their overall grades. If students have worked in teams, they also complete a peer assessment for each member of their team. I then average the team score to input as one grade in my grade book. The important part about individual and team reflections is requiring students to provide an explanation for their scoring decisions. Written evidence of a score is necessary to ensure student honesty. At this point, it is also important to have students set a goal for improvement in upcoming Authentic Learning Experiences.

Final Thoughts

Grading is a reality in the educational system. Unfortunately, there is no end in sight for attaching a grade to any completed work that a student produces. However, through incorporating Authentic Learning Experiences in the classroom, it is possible to "bring the joy back into assessment," as my colleague and friend Erika Jordan often says. Including continuous formative assessment throughout the Authentic Learning Experience will allow you to almost predict the summative assessment outcome for each student. Relying more on student engagement in the process and less on the threat of an end-of-the-unit test that is focused on memorization of content will be a more joyful experience for you and your students.

CHAPTER 9

— ■ —

Facilitating Authentic Learning Experiences

Let's face it: Many teachers prefer to be the center of attention and like to take charge. I am certainly no exception! The first several years of my career reflect this. While I incorporated many student-centered learning strategies, there was nothing more satisfying than a perfectly delivered speech with easy-to-understand outlined notes on the overhead projector. After a few years passed, these notes eventually transitioned into beautiful PowerPoint slides with carefully chosen graphics for enhancement. I loved to hear myself talk. My master's thesis was even titled "The Effective Use of Lecture in the Classroom." However, upon my own professional reflection, I can honestly say that many of my students weren't nearly as enthused as I was with this methodology. In fact, if I truly want to be honest with myself, much of my attraction to the lecture method was based on the mere fact that I struggled to come up with any other ideas on how best to teach my students the content of my courses. Sure, I incorporated what I considered student-centered learning through simulations and activities, but lecture was the easiest way for me to expose my students to the content. When it came time for the end-of-the-unit test and my students didn't necessarily perform as well as I wanted, I had to convince myself that it wasn't my fault. I had told them all they needed to know. Who was I kidding?

Creating a classroom environment conducive to Authentic Learning Experiences can be unsettling. It is counterintuitive to our educational training, and to many administrators, it may look out of control. There are even times when you may feel out of control! However, if you dig deeper, you will find that students are in fact learning, mastering content, thinking critically, and practicing the art of communication throughout the process. So how do we ensure these skills are developing and the content is at the forefront of the learning?

After reading the various chapters on how to design Authentic Learning Experiences for your students, don't get so excited that you throw out all the great teaching tools and lessons that you have created over the years! Instead, think of ways in which you can use these tools and lessons to support the Authentic Learning Experience. Remember, you are still the most critical component in the successful execution of the experience, and yes, you still can incorporate a short lecture or two when direct instruction is needed. However, a shift in the thinking of how you might approach your day-to-day classroom strategies might be necessary.

As you think about the implementation process of Authentic Learning Experiences, start with the experience itself as the core focus of the students' learning. Everything that you will integrate over the course of the experience should be specifically designed to support that experience. Your understanding of this process may be enhanced if you visualize the transformation that took place in my own classroom.

Before I started designing Authentic Learning Experiences for my students, I had separate lessons for each day. They followed best practices and a design that would make Madeline Hunter proud, with anticipatory sets, guided practice, independent practice, and closure. However, they were simply separate lessons that had no connection to one another. Sure, they may have focused on an overall unit theme such as the Great Depression, but that was the only connection. Once my students were "ready" to take the end-of-the-unit test, I wondered why they performed at a lower standard than I would have liked. In the analysis of my own practice, I determined it was because the connection between the lessons was so weak. Thus, in creating an Authentic Learning Experience, now all the mini-lessons, activities, simulations, debates, research, and even (gasp) test prep is focused on the connection to that experience. I like to think that I still make Hunter proud through my implementation process; however, the process is evident throughout the Authentic Learning Experience, rather than in a separate daily implementation.

Taking the First Steps

To begin an Authentic Learning Experience, you must start with a way in which to engage your students. The Buck Institute for Education (www.bie. org) calls this an Entry Event, and it has some great information on how to design these. I would encourage you to check out some of their resources to use in tandem with Authentic Learning Experiences. However, if you truly want to make this an Authentic Learning Experience, you have to move beyond mock letters written by a pretend interested party. Remember, if this experience is going to be authentic, you have to make the start of the experience real! The Buck Institute for Education's *PBL Starter Kit* (Larmer, 2009) notes that field trips, guest speakers, the use of startling statistics, or even video clips can engage and energize students in preparation for the work ahead. The caveat is to choose wisely. What will engage your students the most? What do you have direct access to for implementation? While it might not be feasible to invite an expert into your classroom for a face-to-face meeting with your students, you might be able to Skype with that expert instead. Maybe it is cost prohibitive for you to take a field trip to excite your students, but a Google Earth tour as a virtual field trip could be a substitute. While a live performance by a group of artists would be sure to entice any student, you may have to resort to a video of a performance. Whatever the case, please just don't start the Authentic Learning Experience by telling the students about the challenging investigation and explaining the rubric that accompanies it!

> ☑ **Check for Understanding**
>
> Choose one of the featured Authentic Learning Experiences in the previous chapters, and design three potential ways in which you could introduce the experience. Present the overview of the experience at your next department meeting, and take an informal poll about your ideas. Conduct a discussion regarding the pros and cons of each idea.

Once you have engaged your students in the Authentic Learning Experience upon which they are about to embark, it is now time for students to devise a plan of attack. Conduct a guided brainstorming session, as discussed in Chapter 4, where students begin to lay out the steps they will need to take in order to solve the challenging investigation. This session could take place online with older students if you have the technology in place in your classroom. I would also suggest placing students into smaller groups for approximately ten minutes before sharing out with the whole class to create a master plan. Keep in mind, this is to be used as a guide for students, and once the students become invested in the learning process, they may find the need to modify the plan to fit their needs. During this brainstorming process, it is also important that you, the teacher, lead the students in the beginning stages of their learning. Feel free to question them, challenge their ideas, and steer the conversation as needed. Remember, you are the facilitator and you have an important role. However, while you want to ensure students are beginning this journey with a definite focus, you don't want to dissuade them either. Key questions to incorporate could include, "What might be the result of such an action?" or "What additional information might we need to discover?" In short, encourage, focus, and direct, but don't take over.

As your students become entrenched in the Authentic Learning Experience, it is necessary to continue to guide them. Therefore, having specific criteria that must be met or included in the mastery of the standards and communicating that criteria is paramount to ensuring a successful experience. Depending on your own comfort level with the implementation process and the culture that you have built in your own classroom, you may or may not involve your students in this process. Certainly, you are the subject matter expert, and you know the standards that must be included, thus you should have a preconceived idea of the criteria, even if you are going to involve your students in this process. I find it helpful to create a checklist of the requirements that the students, and I, can refer to throughout the execution of the experience. It is also a good idea to create guiding or focus questions that fall under the overarching challenging investigation (see Figure 9.1, page 151). These questions can be implemented as part of your formative assessments and are helpful in creating the day-to-day lessons that may need to be scaffolded for your students.

Giving students a rubric for outcomes and expectations is also appropriate at this juncture. You can choose to have student input in this process as well. I, however, find it helpful to prevent "rubric fatigue" and simply repurpose my rubrics. This is also helpful for ensuring that students know what to expect. I do shy away from providing students with models of what I anticipate the final outcome to look like. In some cases, this is because the experience is one that we are implementing for the first time and I don't have any models! In other instances, I don't want students to start the experience with a vision of the right answer, since, if the experience has been designed properly, there isn't one right answer.

Figure 9.1   Guiding and Focus Questions

CHALLENGING INVESTIGATION	POSSIBLE GUIDING OR FOCUS QUESTIONS
How can we create a more effective set of emergency procedures for implementation in our school?	▪ How are evacuation routes designed? ▪ What are the legal implications of executing emergency plans in public areas? ▪ How were major historical disaster events handled in relation to implemented emergency procedures?
How can we design and build a new bridge for the local township park that will cross the area's wetland?	▪ How do engineers determine the highest strength-to-weight ratio design? ▪ How do potential bridge loads influence the design of the bridge? ▪ How does traffic flow impact bridge design?
How can we persuade more students to carpool when driving to school?	▪ What is the average historical cost analysis of driving versus carpooling over the last twenty years? ▪ What are the negative environmental effects of increased vehicle usage? ▪ What type of legislative action can be taken to support this endeavor?

Collaboration Is a Needed Skill

The question of collaboration and how to team students is always at the forefront of the minds of teachers when authentic or project work is discussed. Do students really have to work in teams? What happens if students don't share the work equally? Why can't students work alone? These are all great questions, and the answers to them really depend on the design of the Authentic Learning Experience.

Collaboration has been identified as a 21st-century skill. However, I wonder why collaboration has been considered something of importance just since the turn of the century! Haven't we always needed the skill, whether on the battlefield, on the playing field, or in most professional fields? So, of course, collaboration should be a part of an Authentic Learning Experience. However, it is not necessary to create an experience for students that requires them to work in teams. Collaboration can come in many different forms.

I am writing this book alone. I'm not working with a partner or as part of a team effort. However, I am collaborating in other ways. I have sought out teachers to showcase, and this book would not be what it is without them. I am working with a publisher. I have colleagues who have reviewed my manuscript. All of these are forms of collaboration, but at the most basic level it has been me in my pajamas late at night (and sometimes during the day too), working on my writing. This is an authentic experience for me, and there are plenty of other authentic experiences that happen to us on a daily basis that require us to work independently but at some juncture also require a collaboration of sorts. Thus, it is perfectly acceptable to create an Authentic Learning Experience for your students that requires a great deal of independence. However, at some point in the process, students need to collaborate with others. This collaboration might come in the form of peer editing and feedback, or it might come from experts in the field with whom your students have worked in a mentoring capacity. Remember, feedback and reflecting can be difficult for students to process, as it is often evidence of shortcomings. The value, however, is in realizing the power of revision once we have reflected on that feedback and how much better the work can become as a result of it.

While an independent focus might be taken in one Authentic Learning Experience, once you are ready to tackle multiple experiences for your students, it is certainly advisable to create team efforts for some experiences. The size and makeup of the team might look very different from experience to experience. It will all depend on the design, focus, and requirements of the experience. I have had students work with partners, in groups of three or four, and even in groups of ten when a lack of resources dictated the size. I have also designed experiences that require students to start in smaller groups of four to present their original ideas for the challenging investigation. These smaller-group presentations then lead to a class discussion on the best solution, which then becomes the focus for a full-class presentation to an expert panel.

Researching

It is inevitable that research will need to be conducted by your students as they immerse themselves in the process of solving the challenging investigation. However, research can easily take a huge chunk of time. Additionally, the researching skills of students can vary greatly. Once I had a student spend twenty minutes reading a website that discussed York County, South Carolina, when she should have been researching York County, Pennsylvania! Thus, it is necessary to direct the focus of the students' research. Again, depending on your access to technology, you could create a list of sites that you share with your students via a social bookmarking site. My favorites that I regularly incorporate are Delicious and Diigo. You could also create a Google Custom Search Engine for your students, which is particularly beneficial for limiting search results and is great for upper elementary and middle school students, as well as high school students who need the extra support. Additionally, if you are fortunate enough to have a district that will pay for it, tap into the power of using netTrekker. Students are able to search sites that are already teacher approved and are ranked according to readability levels. However, if technology is a prohibitive factor in your district, there is nothing wrong with asking your school librarian to pull the resources from the library shelves. It is also a great idea to take your students to the library the first week of school for a refresher lesson on how to use any available databases that your district has purchased. This will save you time later on as your students begin their researching.

Scaffolding Is Not Differentiation

During the researching and acquisition phase, you are still going to need to incorporate a variety of scaffolding activities. However, remember that scaffolding is not necessarily a process of differentiation for students. Scaffolding focuses on chunking the learning for students and supporting them through the Authentic Learning Experience. Thus, leaving students on their own to merely research is ill-advised and can lead to an end product that is not worthy of your outside audience. Having students reflect on their research at regular intervals will help you to monitor and adjust as needed. Journaling, either online or on paper, is an excellent way to determine next steps for both you and your students. I prefer to have my students keep a daily journal in which they respond to the challenging investigation and continually add to their knowledge base. My review of these entries helps me to fill in gaps as needed and plan for small-group and whole-group lessons. Keep in mind, however, this daily journaling process must become a part of the culture of the classroom. Don't be surprised if your students at first tell you, "We just answered this question yesterday"! Simply gently remind them that the question is so open-ended that they can't possibly answer it in full with a short reflective response in their journal. In time, they will find journaling to be as useful as you do.

Small-group and large-group instruction is an integral part of my daily routine and helps me to scaffold for my students. Sure, there are some days that are completely dedicated to "project" work. However, if every day were reserved for project work, you and your students would not be getting as much out of the Authentic Learning Experience as you should. Through ongoing formative assessment, as noted in Chapter 8, I am able to determine which students I need to target in reference to understanding specific

Figure 9.2   Five Tips to Remember

- Support researching efforts.
- Daily reflection on the challenging investigation through formalized journaling is important.
- Incorporate small-group instruction.
- Scaffolding isn't set in stone but is dictated by formative assessment outcomes.
- Differentiation makes all the difference in ensuring student success.

content and meeting the goals of our standards. I always make small groups an option, and I have my regular small-group "junkies" who attend nearly every session. However, I can easily suggest, cajole, or persuade any student to attend when needed. Using small groups as an option gives students a sense of empowerment over their own learning. It also helps you to differentiate as needed for your students. This is always a powerful opportunity to make students feel like they are not lost in the larger crowd of the class. More individualization can be applied at this level, and those students who are frequently quiet in a larger group have the occasion to have their voices heard. Small groups can meet as often as is needed, but in a block-scheduled class, I typically incorporate small groups three times a week. Additionally, I give students the option to request small-group topics. I plan for small groups around topics that I know typically challenge students, but allowing them to have an additional say in what they need support on is simply one more way in which students become the directors of their own learning. During the small-group instruction, incorporating anything from primary-source analysis to extra math-problem practice can take place.

There are times during the Authentic Learning Experience when it is appropriate to integrate a full-class mini-lesson or activity. Again, this is part of the scaffolding process. Including anything that supports the process of student understanding and acquisition of the content and mastery of the standards is appropriate here. However, "giving" the students too much of the information and providing them with the "right answer" is counterintuitive to the Authentic Learning Experience. While it is perfectly acceptable to conduct a mini-lecture lesson, before doing so, ask yourself if it is truly necessary in the learning process. Otherwise, you may find your attempt at the Authentic Learning Experience has been hampered by your effort to ensure students are getting the "right" information instead of allowing students to uncover the natural connections among the content. Figure 9.2 (above) summarizes the important things that we've discussed in this chapter.

Final Thoughts

Facilitating Authentic Learning Experiences can be a challenging shift in your teaching practice. As teachers, we are so ingrained with the need to tell our students the right answer and to prepare them for standardized tests. However, there is no comparison between "teaching" students and "guiding" students. Helping students to discover a passion for learning and the drive to attack challenging problems head-on is one of the most important facets in the world of education. While we certainly cannot sit passively in the back of the room as students plan their first solo trek, we can make the most of our expertise as we build the appropriate bridges to span the gaps in learning and support the structure as the students connect the building blocks.

REFERENCES

Angela Zhang, High school student devises potential cancer cure. (2012, January 15).
    The Huffington Post. Retrieved from http://www.huffingtonpost.com/2012/01/15/
    angela-zhang-high-school-_n_1207177.html

Breaker. (n.d.). Project Breaker. Retrieved from http://www.projectbreaker.org/about/

Claims for the English language arts/literacy summative assessment. (2012, March
    1). Smarter Balanced Assessment Consortium. Retrieved from http://www.
    smarterbalanced.org/wordpress/wp-content/uploads/2012/09/Smarter-Balanced-
    ELA-Literacy-Claims.pdf

Claims for the mathematics summative assessment. (2012, May 18). Smarter Balanced
    Assessment Consortium. Retrieved from http://www.smarterbalanced.org/
    wordpress/wp-content/uploads/2012/09/Smarter-Balanced-Mathematics-Claims.
    pdf

CyberFair 2013. (n.d.). Global SchoolNet. Retrieved from http://www.globalschoolnet.
    org/gsncf.

InnoCentive Challenges. (n.d.). InnoCentive. Retrieved from http://innocentive.com/ar/
    challenge/browse

Larmer, J. (2009). *PBL starter kit.* Novato, CA: Buck Institute for Education.

National Governors Association Center for Best Practices, Council of Chief State School
    Officers (2010). Common Core State Standards Initiative. Washington D.C.:
    National Governors Association Center for Best Practices, Council of Chief State
    School Officers.

Parry, W. (2011, May 12). Teen discovers promising cystic fibrosis treatment. *Live
    Science.* Retrieved from http://www.livescience.com/14138-teen-cystic-fibrosis-
    drug-cocktail-contest.html

What Is GIS? (n.d.). Esri. Retrieved from www.esri.com/what-is-gis.

What We Do. (n.d.). InnoCentive. Retrieved from http://www.innocentive.com/about-
    innocentive

An environmentally friendly book printed and bound in England by www.printondemand-worldwide.com

This book is ma~~~~~~naterials for the text pages.

#0326 - 280116 - C0 - 254/178/9 - PB - 9781596672451